CONQUERING THE SEVEN C'S

for Better Face-to-Face and Online Teaching

JASON J. PUGH

DEDICATION

This manuscript is dedicated to:

My wife, April, who has been my anchor throughout every challenge presented. She has been encouraging, loving, and unwaveringly supportive throughout every step of the journey. I could not have written this without her inspiration.

Also, to my four daughters: Tonnie, Emmalyn, Ashlee, and Maisie (TEAM Pugh), all of whom remind me to stay grounded and grateful for everything I have. Thank you, TEAM Pugh, for being such an incredible family.

Conquering the Seven C's

for Better Face-to-Face and Online Teaching

©2021 Jason J. Pugh

print ISBN: 978-1-09836-729-9

CONTENTS

INTRODUCTION:
GETTING READY FOR THE VOYAGE AHEAD

Teaching various types of learners is not like kicking your feet up on a cruise ship; it is more like being on a pirate ship that takes on water, hits massive waves, and faces outside natural elements, all at once. Many students either do not have the time to grasp new ideas, lack flexibility in sitting down and learning something new, or possess a level of self-doubt that they might not know as much as they think they know. Throw in the mix of today's ever-changing learning modalities, preparation of new relevant material, and high standards of keeping engagement for a day or a week at a time.

With the recent shift in technology, learning remotely has become more prevalent than ever. More and more students have decided to learn in a live online environment. Teachers and educators alike have had to prepare material, find and operate online platforms (both synchronous and asynchronous) effectively, and still be able to engage students at a high level so that topics are engaging and meaningful. Simply put, it is like being a one-man crew, and you are probably questioning how the ship didn't sink yet.

You. It is because of you and your ability to engage adult learners into taking a leap of faith and trying something new. If you teach adult learners, you know the benefits that stand out: The feedback from evaluations, the promotions you see they received on LinkedIn, the thank you notes that come in, and more.

Still, these massive changes in adult education beg the question: How do we meet the demands of students who learn a million different ways in several different modalities?

The answer is simple and complex all at the same time: Regardless of modality, the best teachers can truly teach anything to anyone. Yes, there are differences in teaching in an online setting compared to a Face-to-Face (F2F) environment that require changes in the way we approach learning and teaching in different platforms. However, if educators possess the right tools and practice using the modality diligently, they can be able to achieve wonders during instruction and facilitation.

I must stress this: THIS BOOK IS NOT JUST FOR K-12 EDUCATORS! The "C's" in this book can be applied to educators who teach any students from five to eighty-five. These can work for those who teach, train, demonstrate products, and even sell. These concepts are universal in approach, but you can associate these "C's" to your direct teaching practices and the environments you manage.

For this book, training and teaching are used synonymously, even though they have slightly different meanings. Teaching is the concept of shaping minds to think differently. Training is the idea of increasing knowledge and skill to be more productive. This book aims to readjust the standard of the word training to do both: Allow you to sharpen your existing skills, while shaping your mind to open and utilize the right tools in your practices.

Abraham Maslow once said, "I suppose it is tempting, if the only tool you have is a hammer, to treat everything as if it were a nail." Over the last fifteen years, I have taught in K-12 settings, post-secondary settings, small business, and corporate environments. I have dedicated my entire career toward mastering asynchronous and synchronous approaches toward more meaningful learning, engagement, and depth. I have taught online, face-to-face, hybrid, blended, and any other technological manner considered. I have gathered useful screwdrivers, wrenches, pliers, clamps, and more. My mission is to teach you how to use these tools effectively so that you know how and when to utilize them for the right situations.

The tools provided come in the form of concepts. Each of the concepts provided allows you to reflect, practice, and further engage in teaching, regardless of an F2F or an online setting. There will be variations discussed throughout this book as to how each concept can be used in either setting (as there are differences). Your goal is to acquire each of the concepts, then spread them to every student you encounter.

I called this book *Conquering the Seven C's* because each concept ensures that you will successfully navigate the next steps of your voyage in teaching. Each "C" must be practiced independently, yet they are building blocks from each previous "C."

The seven "C's", divided into three sections, follows the premise of an adventure to higher learning. We will call each of these sections "Our Voyages." I must warn you that there will be heavy currents, rocky waves, storms, and several different elements that will rock your ship. However, when you find and have the power of learning each C, you will possess a characteristic of education that is unswerving in its power.

To accomplish this successfully, we are going to investigate the challenges, techniques, and approaches for each "C" we travel. There will be additional appendices to be your maps, and a compass to guide you toward your own direction. Let's view each of the "C's" associated with our Voyages. The Voyages you will embark are The Voyage Inward, The Voyage Outward, and The Voyage Beyond.

Section 1: The Voyage Inward

1st C: *Command* (Of Self and Values)

2nd C: *Change* (The Current Mindset)

3rd C: *Confidence* (In Efficacy of Practice)

Section 2: The Voyage Outward

> 4th C: *Captivation* (Of Your Audience's Attention)
>
> 5th C: *Clarity* (In Message and Meaning)
>
> 6th C: *Connection* (With Every Individual)

Section 3: The Voyage Beyond

> 7th C: *Completeness* (In Instruction; No Wave Left Unconquered)

The Voyages Ahead

These voyages will require you to look inward, then look outward, and lastly try to see beyond the horizon for best teaching practices that will work for you. The first voyage is a deep-dive inward to gather your teaching inventory. These will be the hardest "C's" to conquer because it will require you to fully comprehend your greatest strengths, goals, ambitions, values, weaknesses, pain points, and paradigms. The Voyage Inward is a dark one; it requires pure honesty in failed practices, true confidence in the successful traits you possess, and a moral compass to recognize and utilize both when necessary.

When you sail, you should know how to command the wheel. When you teach, it is the exact same, only your wheel is your values and your style. You should also know that you are going to need to shift direction and change some things in your current mindset to avoid the big storms. You also need to know how to confidently showcase your old and new skills without coming off as arrogant or pompous. The Voyage Inward is your toughest voyage, and from there, it should become a bit easier.

The second voyage, or the Voyage Outward, requires that you possess the ability to make an impact on others. This voyage will teach you to ensure that your ship stays its course, to keep all of your guests entertained, to navigate through choppy waters when problems arise, and to consistently stay firm and strong with communication of direction and information. It requires you to be the captain: The one who leads others. These "C's" will catapult you into instructional leadership and ensures that you make sure every passenger enjoys the voyage by being captivating, clear, consistent, calm, and connective with the people aboard.

The final voyage is one that goes beyond, the ever-lasting search for completeness. It is the one that keeps us fighting to be the best captains we can be. This will take a long time to complete, but the voyage itself is the advantage because you are staying active in pursuing as much knowledge, insight, research, instructional tips, feedback, and openminded methodologies as possible.

The final voyage is a quest that does not end. I know that may sound a bit terrifying because we all look for a sense of completeness in our teaching practices. Do not be afraid of this. The best educators always look for self-growth and gaining more meaning in their teaching. If you are positively unwavering in your currently abilities, yet still open to learning more holistically, then that completeness occurs more naturally in your pursuit of engaging instruction. It is all about being comfortable in knowing what you have to offer, but always looking for the next adventure in your learning and growth.

The final 'C' is all about attitude; it is meant to have us continuously looking to become the most complete form of ourselves as educators. To be honest, I am still on the voyage beyond, even as I write this. There are new skills, practices, approaches, theories, and applications that I learn. I don't just search for these new concepts; I embrace them. I love the thrill of leaving no wave undiscovered and becoming a master of the open sea that is teaching others. I hope that by the end of this book, you also seek the thrill that is the newest approach, method, or skill in teaching other people how to be the best.

I must stress this key concept when voyaging on the Seven "C's." It is perfectly okay if your current practices are not immediately amazing after reading this book. It takes a ton of practice, effort, energy, reflection, and adjustments to hone your skills and teach the way that is best for you. Your goal is to use this as a cyclical reminder of the voyages you have been on, the current voyage, and the goal for future voyages. This book is not a "read and put on the bookshelf forever" kind of book. It is meant to be picked up again and again for current reflection when you need it.

Another hidden beauty of these "C's" is that they function slightly differently for everyone. What you will gain out of this book might look different from your fellow instructors, co-teachers, mentors, mentees, principals, managers, and leaders. My advice is this: Read it alone and share together! You can do this after each "C," each Voyage, or after the entire book. Just read and share. I always find that learning about yourself and being able to share your findings allows doors for confirmation or adjustments from your fellow team members. It also allows you to create more meaningful open dialogue with the people who know you best in your profession.

One final token to remember: Although it is a good thing to focus on a destination of being an amazing educator, the voyage is more important. In this book, you will find these three voyages will teach you how to be more effective in your practices and makes the destination all more worthwhile.

Are you ready for the voyages that await? If so, I cannot wait to have some fun with you as we hit the open waters! But first, we should probably check to make sure our ship is properly prepared and has received the right maintenance in advance.

CHAPTER 1:
PREPARING THE SHIP

It is extremely difficult to sail a ship without understanding the territory that lies ahead and tools you must use to navigate it. Much like having a map, compass, and crew to help you in your preparation, in teaching you to know where you are going, ensure you are staying on the right path, and know who your lines of support are throughout the process.

Preparing your ship is an arduous task because it requires you to fully reflect on what is working (and not working) and understand the types of people (waters) you encounter. Without this preparation, though, your ship would most assuredly sink. Education of any kind is a craft and requires a knowledge of your current inventory of skills, your areas of growth that are needed, and enough understanding to have the confidence to employ them gracefully in your environment. Furthermore, it is equally important to know how to navigate when working in an online platform versus a training at a particular location, as the waters change dramatically in the preparation.

There are several differences in teaching in a F2F setting versus an online platform that must be explored. First, when teaching in a F2F setting, you must know several facets of the territory. This includes the point of contact of the location, the expectations of the contact and their students, the environment itself (projectors, tv's, plug-ins, laptop vs. their computer, internet access), and how the environment is set up for students (round table, conference style, large or small room). The advantage of teaching in a F2F setting is that you know what you are getting. If you ask your contact the right questions, the chances of future issues occurring reduce greatly. However, the disadvantage is that if you do not ask the right questions, you are left fumbling and if students witness this, you are already down a notch before the beginning of your presentation.

In contrast, online environments allow for less contact to be made because normally there is a Learning Management System (LMS) in place to show you enrollments and inform you of what platform you will be using for instruction. In addition, most organizations use the same online teaching platform for many different trainings.

For synchronous learning, this could include Adobe Connect, WebEx, GoToWebinar, Zoom, Blackboard Collaborate, Microsoft Teams, or others. The disadvantage is that you not only need to familiarize yourself with the platforms and all the instruments they provide to aid instruction, you need to also understand how you best fit into an online instruction model.

After teaching in several different modalities over the last decade and a half, I have taken some bumps and bruises because of the environment I encountered. Rather than share a bunch of horror stories of moving too fast (teaching the Online Pictures feature for Microsoft Excel and having a typo in the description, only leading to a non-fully clothed individual displayed on an 80" TV screen) to accidentally emphasizing the importance of "Titter" (NOT Twitter) on a recorded session for lawyers, I would rather inform you that no matter how much you practice, mistakes are going to be made. The question is this: How do you navigate from there? True education is about how we roll with the punches and still stay confident when those mistakes occur.

Preparing with The CYA Model (No, Not that CYA!)

I want to remind you that the number of mistakes can be reduced greatly when the right preparation occurs. Through all my years of education, I have simplified preparation into three major tiers, appropriately nicknamed,

"CYA." These stand for preparing and mastering your *Content*, *Yourself*, and your *Audience*. Although the name might not be the most politically correct, the approach to mastering each of the three components are critical toward an educator's success. Each of these tiers work like cogs in a wheel; without one, the other two will not spin successfully.

Figure 1: The CYA Model of Preparation

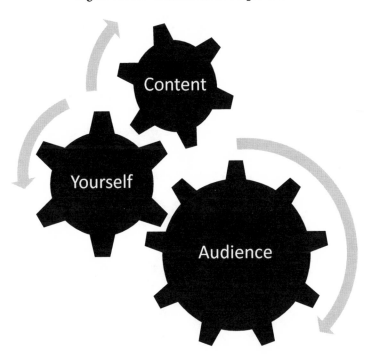

The CYA Model of Preparation is something I utilize before I ever teach in an online or F2F classroom. Knowing what content you are going to deliver, how you are going to ensure the students are grasping what you are delivering, and who you are impacting in your delivery turns a decent educator into a powerful one. Each cog has multiple components, or parts, that require questioning, analysis, and thorough practice. Think of these as considerations you must make and ensure that you feel 100% confident in the approach you are going to take in your teaching practices. To gain that confidence and become a powerful educator, please carry this thought always: If you don't prepare effectively, you won't engage the people you teach.

Preparing Content

The first tier of preparation is a more obvious one. As an educator, it is crucial that you prepare your content and become an expert of the topic. There are many people who mention that "sometimes you have to fake it until you make it." I personally do not believe in this philosophy. Yes, if you are new to teaching or training, there are going to be some components that you are going to have to pretend to master along the way. However, the more equity and investment you spend on mastering the knowledge and application content inside and out, the better your overall performance will be.

In my experience as an educator and a leader of educators, I have gathered and consistently prepared four components of content before teaching. It is imperative that you should practice these components and attempt to master them. These four components are *substance, elaboration, relevant examples,* and *real-world application. Substance* is the meat of the content; it is meant to show that you have a full grasp of the content you are teaching. *Elaboration* is the component that allocates more rich synthesis into the topic so that exploration is available for the student to ask questions. *Relevant examples* allow you to create the bridge of what you know to how the students can also know the information. Lastly, *real-world application* allows the student to begin employing the content into their daily lives and provides an arena for them to practice the skills they are trying to gain.

All four of these components work in harmony, so that you can dive deeper with the subject matter and ensure your students not only understand it, but also practice and apply it in their daily routines. For example, if you are teaching a concept on understanding the importance of using AutoSum in a professional Microsoft Excel course, you should easily be able to provide the following to the students you are teaching:

- *Substance*: An AutoSum feature allows you to quickly add a total number for a range of cells together, without typing a formula or manually typing the cells for an associated range. It provides an easier way for you to calculate numbers efficiently, without executing a lot of steps.

- *Elaboration:* To accomplish this easily, simply place your mouse cursor in the cell immediately below the range of cells you would like to add. Then, navigate to the Home tab, in the top-right group called Editing, and select the AutoSum button. Here you will notice the range has been automatically added without having to type in the formula.

- *Relevant Example:* For example, let's say you needed to add up a range of monthly sales totals for a particular branch or location. You can enter the numbers in each of the cells from cells A1 through A12. Then, when you place your cursor in cell A13 and click AutoSum, the totals add up and now you have a yearly total.

- *Real-World Application:* You could apply this to many settings in your work areas. You could use this to add expenses, finances, budgets, sales, hourly payroll totals, and so much more.

The next time you are preparing your content, ask yourself if you can properly educate and provide meaningful understanding to your students by providing a case for each of those four components. You will find that if you cannot provide any of those four components, you should review the content again until mastery has been achieved. I must stress this: You do not need to know 100% of the answers, but 100% of the answers you provide must be shared with confidence and accuracy. To properly test yourself, ask questions that you think may appear. When you are teaching your students, quickly jot questions that begin to repeat because something is missing in your content preparation. You may find a valuable pattern that you need to better prepare when you teach the next set of students.

Notice that in the CYA Model of Preparation, this cog is the smallest in the moving components because it is a skill that is normally learned first in your education classes. Professors and fellow educators drill the *Content* component during your pre-teaching years to ensure that you know your content inside and out. This book will discuss the first four components of *Content* at times, but this is something that good educators use when they prepare every lesson, so it will not be a focal point. There are several industry resources to help you develop your content knowledge more strongly.

The key questions I choose to ask are these: If every student that becomes an educator is drilled to know their content inside and out, then why aren't all educators considered elite in their teaching practices? What pieces are missing that turn a good educator into an elite educator? The answer lies in the next two components of the CYA Model of Preparation.

Preparing Yourself

What you prepare is very important and can make you a decent educator. *How you prepare* is one of the major pieces that makes you a great educator. There are many teachers, educators, facilitators, and instructors I have worked with over the years that knew their content inside and out, but their delivery consistently missed the mark and left students confused, bored, or even worse, completely disengaged. Knowing, practicing, and mastering your own individual teaching style is vital for teaching success, and will be the key focal point in the next few chapters during The Voyage Inward. It is imperative that we understand, recognize, and practice the aspects of preparing yourself appropriately before delivering a lesson.

Preparing yourself can also be broken into four different components. These components are *delivery, style, transparency,* and *modality*. First, with *delivery*, you must recognize the importance of expectations, transitioning from topic to topic, and how the lessons are approached. I think of delivery as a form of engagement, as in being able to approach learning from five different avenues. This includes using cooperative learning, question and answer, whole-group lecture, hands-on, or small group breakouts.

When you prepare yourself and your delivery methods, you should learn how to transition lessons amongst all five approaches and be able to utilize each method where the time serves appropriately. There will be times where you are introducing a new concept and whole-group lecture is going to be the right delivery method. Then you are going to need to shift dramatically into an activity where you will have the students shift into groups of four and have them inquire new approaches or practice new strategies that they just learned.

The question is: Can you do this effectively? If not, the amount or recognition and practice must be repeated until mastery is complete. To become a master of this, you must become a student yourself and learn about each of these approaches and what types of strategies can be used for each. The best advice is to learn one, practice using activities and building lessons with it, and see where potential issues may arise. Then, when you feel one is mastered, move to the next.

The next component is *style*. Style is the unique approach taken that allows you to be *you*. This is where you get to decide the type of educator you are going to be. Are you going to be humorous? Serious? Dramatic? Emphatic? Loud? Soft?

I must admit that if you have ever met me, the first thing you would think is that I am a loud giant. I have a very boisterous, enthusiastic, showman-like personality. I have cheesy dad-jokes, a goofy persona, but can flip a switch immediately to be serious when I need to truly drive a meaningful point home to my audience. That is my style. Your personality should shine through as your teaching style. Once again, it takes a lot of reflection, desire, and repetition to gain that level of comfort in knowing who you are in front of your audience.

My best piece of advice for finding your style is this: Be authentic. Be genuine. Be real. The audience can sniff through a fake, canned-voice presenter. They appreciate someone who is confident in the delivery and authentic in the way he or she shares meaningful information with them. Many writers and teachers will say to develop a "teaching voice." I disagree. Develop your own voice that can resonate with your audience, capture their attention, and get them to think and feel during your lesson. More on this later...

Next, it is crucial to know how *transparent* you are going to be about revealing yourself to your audience. Some educators are amazing presenters because they have a raw, open style where they let the audience into their lives as they are teaching. They will share information about their children, spouses, hobbies, and additional insights to connect with their students. To me, this is the best approach to take.

Other educators will leave their life behind and only reveal a small bit about themselves. I have also seen this work as well, but the reason why is because they are so focused on having a strong demonstration that their transparency does not have to be as open. Either way, you must take an in-depth view of how open you want to be about yourself to your audience.

Lastly, you must know how you are going to teach in the *modality* used. In 21st century learning, more and more teaching arenas are being presented. How are you going to teach at a client's conference room site in a F2F setting? Do you know to bring your own laptop, or will they have a computer there? Do you need to bring a flash drive? What about internet hook-up? These are questions you ask even before you begin your first word of the lesson.

From there, you also should consider these points: How much am I going to move around the room? How much eye contact should I make with each individual? Should I remember everyone's name, or do I need name tents? Each of these approaches are critical in the way you present to adults or children in a face-to-face environment. It takes solid, confident decision-making and it also takes the will to go valiantly with whatever you decide.

Conversely, what if you are teaching in an online platform? So many different factors need to be considered in this modality. The type of platform, whether there will be a questions panel, participants panel, additional features you can utilize to engage your audience, audio checks, and being able to teach the students to use the platform from a students' perspective all become massive factors in the way you are going to teach. Not to mention, each platform has its own hurdles to consider. The best advice here is to go online and review what options each online platform has to offer and then decide how your delivery methods and teaching style are going to work best with that platform.

Preparing for Your Audience

We have discussed the importance of preparing what you teach and how you teach, but there is still a third component still needs to be addressed: Preparing for who you teach. This is the key principle behind the second set of chapters ahead, titled The Voyage Outward. Knowing and preparing for the types of students you are going to encounter for each class will make the biggest difference in the influence of the lesson you provide. Without it, you have no understanding of whether you are truly making an impact or not in your lessons.

In my profession, there are several different types of classes that I teach: Private events, global classes, webinars, question and answer sessions, individualized meeting plans for clients, and trade show demonstrations. Preparing for your audience requires the understanding that students are going to ask several questions on the content. That is only the surface of preparing for your audience appropriately.

Before I teach any type of event, I must fully consider the *engagement, depth, alignment,* and *trust* factors that I am providing to them. These can all vary greatly from class to class. The importance of preparing for each of these components before you teach your audience is essential to gaining their attention, their belief in you and your message, and most importantly, their trust.

First, with *engagement,* we must determine specifically what the audience hopes to achieve by taking a class. If you are teaching a private event in a F2F modality, you must discuss the expected outcomes of taking a class of this nature. Likewise, if you are teaching in an online modality, asking the students to use their microphone, webcam, or chat to explain what their goals are for the class allows for space to be opened and for real discourse to occur. If you are teaching children, you must determine your effective classroom management strategies to ensure you include them in your daily policies. If you are teaching adults, you must find out what their goals and needs are, so you can focus your attention to helping your students achieve them. Regardless of modality or group, if you can identify and prepare for their needs and goals, you can fully comprehend the learners' purpose and identify possible skill gaps in the process.

Even more important than identifying their goals is probing deeper to understand the students' individualized *depth* of their needs. Students will state a goal that may be relatively vague, politically correct, or generalized to show that they have a mission for the class. Being able to decipher between the initial desire vs. their true desire to be better at their professions or coursework is a deeper skill that is not understood immediately. You must ask the probing questions, detailing their specific skill sets, and their potential fears in what they think they might need to do the best job possible.

I primarily teach leadership and development courses and understanding the underlying students' needs is one of the trickiest components because students do not want to feel vulnerable in sharing their weaknesses. When I seek to find a greater depth toward their needs, I normally ask in a way that showcases that the students possess several skills but may hope to achieve new concepts that could make them exceptional at their current role. For example, I engage them immediately by asking what their three biggest strengths are in utilizing a certain topic, and then I ask what three takeaways they would like to grow in regarding that topic. Even if the students provide only two, that is still two more needs that I can address throughout the duration of the class.

This type of approach allows the floor to be opened, a bit more vulnerability to shine through, and essentially promotes richer discussion on their current practices. Metacognition allows them to search deeper within themselves to determine more meaningful areas of growth. This is what *depth* is all about - digging deeper to truly help your learner, regardless of whether they are children or adults.

Once you dive into more *depth*, it is important to understand how you can create *alignment* between your strategies and their needs. This is an opportunity for you to tie the bridge together and show the students how the content you are teaching will apply to their overall benefit in their daily lives. If you have prepped your content effectively and know yourself in the way you are going to deliver the message, the *alignment* should be the easiest component to deliver to the audience at the beginning of a lesson. Objectives should be clearly outlined, stated verbally, and visually shown either in the prior discussion or in the first five minutes of the course being taught. This is a critical step in the process because this is where trust can begin. If a student can believe that the content being taught will help them achieve their individualized goals, then the likelihood for meaningful engagement increases drastically.

Lastly, the importance of *trust* is crucial toward making a meaningful rapport with the audience. First, you must engage with them on the importance of the modality they are using to learn. If they are face-to-face, then you must emphasize expectations, potential breaks and lunch, and seating arrangements to best meet the needs of the class. If they are in an online modality, you must engage with them in how to use communication tools effectively, teach them how to download additional information for the class, and walk them through potential troubleshooting concerns. Discussing breaks are equally important in this environment as well.

Regardless of modality, you must absolutely engage them with the content you are teaching, your teaching style, and what credentials you possess to teach them the content ahead. They need to *trust* who you are, what your motives are, and what you can do for them.

What makes you qualified to teach them? How is your teaching style going to engage them in better learning? What is the content going to do for them? These are all questions that will ultimately provide you with the credibility necessary to have them not only expect but to openly participate in incredible learning from you. If you do not have the credentials, then that means more studying, learning, and being part of more learning-based organizations might be in order. Simply put: The more you know, the more you grow.

Lastly, some scholars may disagree with this next idea, but once again, I believe wholeheartedly in the power of authenticity. I am fully supportive of introducing some personal aspects of your life before you begin. I think it provides a meaningful connection to allow them to know you are human. If you have children, share that you have children. If you have a parakeet, share that too. If you love to hike, do yoga, watch sporting events, go to the opera, or simply watch a show that is hot on TV right now, then do it. This added connection not only provides a level of credibility for you as a professional but reveals a humanistic approach to learning and takes a bit of pressure off of you in being an authoritative figure in the environment you are teaching. Your students will not *trust* you as an expert if they do not *trust* you as a human being first.

I find that preparing for your audience truly permits you to understand whether you are making a meaningful impact in your lessons or not. The sooner you can understand what you audience truly wants from your teaching, the better the overall outcome will be with their retention of what you taught. It takes a lot of effort to individualize needs and goals, but if you do it, and it becomes the focus around your content, you will have your audience hooked on everything you are telling them!

Daily Maintenance of Your Ship

Just like everything else that emphasizes mastery, working on your craft takes a ton of daily maintenance. It requires a certain level of cleaning and polishing until it looks exactly the way you want it. If the CYA Model of Preparation is meant to make sure your sails and mast are working appropriately, the daily maintenance practice is meant to verify that you do not have any holes in your boat. It requires a constant and cyclical element of self-reflection in your teaching practices. It also requires that you have the newest and most up-to-date research and information on the topic you are teaching.

The hardest part about teaching students is that you must force yourself to be your biggest critic and your biggest ally at the same time. If you are truly going to reflect, you must be supportive enough in yourself to know and continue what is working, and you must be strong enough to consider the practices that are not. It requires an internal and data analysis to fully understand what your students, supervisors, leaders, and colleagues say about your teaching practices. It is imperative to make sure that your boat is sturdy and can take on the massive storms, meaning that your emotions are in check when receiving and providing feedback on your teaching practices. This is one of the hardest aspects of teaching because it bruises you internally and forces you to make sure you adjust your daily practices in pursuing excellent teaching. I never said the voyage that lies ahead of you was going to be easy! However, it will be rewarding.

But here is a thought: If you have read this far, you have already demonstrated an innate desire to become the best teacher, educator, instructor, or facilitator that you can be, regardless of modality. The best educators consistently reflect and seek better practices. Every morning, you should take a few minutes to reflect on what you are doing well, what you feel like you can improve, and find the first step in getting started. This could mean seeking an expert resource, reading a book on practice, doing some additional research, or observing others in their practices. The more you are doing to prepare and take care of your ship, the more reliable your ship will be when the waters get rough. Similarly, in Education, the more preparation and practice you do, the better you will become in your teaching practices. You will be better today than you were yesterday, and the day before, and so on.

Caution: There May Be Ship Damage on These Voyages!

The rest of the book focuses on the rough seas that lie ahead. To be upfront with you, there may be some thoughts or insights that are going to rough up your ship. They are going to force you to change your current perspective, analyze the current students that you teach, and seek a sense of accomplishment and completeness in your teaching. The amount of metacognition you will encounter while reading this book will make you think, make you feel, make you cry, make you get angry, or will challenge you to throw everything you are doing away. Let me assure you: This is not my goal.

My goal is not to strip you of the foundations you have built for yourself, much like I would not ask someone to tear down a functional ship and rebuild an entirely new one. I am asking you to prime, paint, repair, and make the necessary adjustments to your teaching practices that might not be working, so that your ship is sturdier and stronger than ever. This does require you to deeply reflect on some of the damaging things that you have done in the past, recognize your warped approaches that might not be working now, and continue the daily maintenance to make sure you are secure and balanced in your reflection and practice.

Now that we fully understand our ship's daily maintenance requirements, the importance of multiple types of preparation, the awareness that our ship may endure a little bit of damage along the way, and we possess the maps for the voyages that await, let's get ready to set sail!

CHAPTER 2:
THE VOYAGE INWARD

On the seas, there are massive obstacles that tend to get in your way. Storms, heavy waves, high winds, and choppy waters will all be prevalent during your trip inward to mastering your teaching craft. There is one thing that I want you to remember while taking this dangerous journey: You are always the captain of your ship!

What does this mean? During the time in the classroom experience (or virtual classroom experience), there are going to be obstacles in your way. These include difficult questions, technology not working, lack of engagement at times, and most importantly the mental, physical, and emotional wear and tear that comes with maintaining excellence in the classroom. Knowing when to push through the waters with your skills and strengths versus knowing when to change the course to save the ship is a crucial skill to have. To do this, you must recognize your *command*, your willingness to *change*, and the *confidence* to decide on when to employ each.

This is what the Voyage Inward is all about: *Identity*. No matter what issues you may run into during your teaching, you must always know your values, strengths, and skills, while being willing to recognize and change what doesn't work. To master these "C's" you must gain recognition of these strengths and weaknesses, then be willing to consistently reflect on those elements to adapt with the times of teaching.

There is only one way you can truly conquer this: Honesty. It is the wheel that guides your ship. You must be honest with yourself, know the values you possess that others do not, and be humble and thick-skinned enough to recognize and change the things that limit mastery.

The Voyage Inward requires you to work through three different "C's" based on this premise of honesty. The first is *command*, which is the mastery of knowing what strengths you have to offer during the delivery of your message. The second is *change*, which is the understanding that you are not perfect, and you must work on the modifications necessary to be an elite educator. The third is *confidence*, which is the belief that you have the power to showcase these strengths in a humble manner and being secure and transparent in those growth points to show objectivity within your teaching practices. Each of the "C's" require a level of depth in your ability to reflect on the way you teach currently.

To be frank, many resources will tell you how to better prepare the content you are teaching. The four pieces on *substance, elaboration, relevant examples*, and *real-world application* are nothing new to the training mind as they are taught and enforced in many college settings, train-the-educator sessions, and teacher workshops. Many educators drill concepts, theories, ideas, practice, and traditional vocabulary for you to be able to teach students in the future. *Content* is always the focus.

However, in Chapter 1, *Content* is the smallest of the cogs in the wheel. I will use the first four components to provide some examples of lessons ahead, but this will not be the emphasis of your ship. If you are reading this book, you are already aware that your content should have relevance, meaning, examples, and application. If they do not, I will help provide these along the way for you, but I would strongly recommend reviewing some workshops, webinars, or other opportunities on teaching various content.

With each of the C's for The Voyage Inward, we are going to ensure maintenance of *your* ship. Therefore, we will further investigate the *Yourself* portions in the CYA table for each "C" in the Voyage Inward. The Voyage

Outward focuses on the Audience component, but it must occur after the first voyage.

Table 1: The CYA Model of Preparation for the Voyage Inward

Content (Already Gained)	Yourself (Voyage Inward)	Audience (Voyage Outward)
Substance	*Delivery*	*Engagement*
Elaboration	*Style*	*Depth*
Relevant Examples	*Transparency*	*Alignment*
Real-World Application	*Modality*	*Trust*

The premise behind The Voyage Inward requires you to thoroughly investigate *how* you are going to teach to your students and what type of educator you want to be. It demands that you to have a firm grasp of the wheel and fully explore where your course on the sea needs to be adjusted. These first three C's are going to be the hardest to endure, but don't worry! I have provided a Captain's Guide for The Voyage Inward at the end of this chapter before you embark on the "C's" ahead of you. This guide will help you assess and reflect on your current internal process when you are teaching, while helping you navigate through the elements that lie ahead. Basically, it is a self-assessment of understanding the educator you currently are and the educator you want to be.

Do you remember the one thing I asked you to do to ensure you have a firm grasp of the wheel? That's right! Be honest with yourself the entire time.

How The Voyage Inward Works

To provide a relevant example (see what I did there?) of understanding The Voyage Inward and to make this content easier to digest, we are going to practice using a current strength that we would see in ourselves and walk through the four steps of knowing yourself. This is how we can best recognize and grow ourselves as educators because it allows us to purely focus on our values and the power that can be applied in the way we share information with others.

For example, let's say I evaluated myself and found that one of my key values is that I am an excellent communicator. The next step I am going to take is to further explore how I am going to enhance my communication skills for each of the *Yourself* components. This is going to allow me to further utilize my strength in the following four components in relation to communication: *Delivery, Style, Transparency,* and *Modality.*

Table 2: Self-Assessment for Teacher Mindset Statements (TMS)

Delivery	*Style*
Yourself: Major Strength or Weakness	
Transparency	*Modality*

For each component, it is truly important that you always keep the strength or weakness in the center, to remind yourself that all areas of knowing yourself surround that strength or weakness. I have provided a *Teacher Mindset Statement, or TMS,* which is a mad-lib of sorts, to help you fully understand the *Yourself* self-evaluation and how it applies directly to your teaching. There are two major types of these TMS's – Strengthening TMS (S-TMS) and Changing TMS (C-TMS).

The S-TMS listed below will help you find more innate qualities than you think. As a result, the ideas for better engagement and management of your teaching practices will grow. This will be discussed more in Chapter 3, which focuses on *command*:

- **If I am/possess/have** _____ *(Strength)*, **I would/should/ can** _____ *(Action that supports strength)* **into my educational lesson to ensure better** _____ *(Delivery/Style/ Transparency/Modality)*. **This will make me a better educator because** _____ *(Reason that supports strength)*.

The C-TMS is more focused on recognizing current educational weaknesses and making actionable changes to ensure better educational delivery, style, transparency, and modality adjustments. I have provided an example for this as well, but you will find this in Chapter 4, which focuses on *change*.

- **If I do not possess/have** _____ *(Strength)*, **I would/should/ can** _____ *(Action that engages change)* **into my educational lesson to ensure better** _____ *(Delivery/Style/ Transparency/Modality)*. **This will make me a better educator because** _____ *(Reason that supports strength)*.

For both types of TMS's, you can add any additional information you feel will help support your reflection. I have provided an example of a *style* component in the *Yourself* cog.

- **S-TMS: If I possess** *dry humor* **in my teaching** *(Strength)*, **I can** *apply more content related jokes that provide light sarcasm (Action that supports strength)* **into my educational lesson to ensure a better** *style (Delivery/Style/Transparency/Modality)*. **This will make me a better educator** *because my students will be more engaged and will be waiting for the next joke to apply. (Reason that supports strength)*.

- **C-TMS: If I do not possess** *dry humor (Strength)*, **I should** *attempt a lighter, sillier humorous anecdote (Action that engages change)* **into my educational lesson to ensure better** *style* **in my teaching.** *(Delivery/Style/Transparency/Modality)*. **This will make me a**

better educator because *it will allow me to adapt and be more flexible and engaging with my students, especially when they do not except it. (Reason that supports strength).*

As you can see, my TMS's for *style* component are very detailed. It has taken multiple practices and revisions for me to get those components where I want to be. They might not be as explicit for you in the beginning, but the idea is that you have the creative space to reflect on what strengths you have.

Also, I should mention that you will not only do this with your greatest strengths, but also with your greatest weaknesses. The TMS's will be similar, but it is more about what you want to decrease in your lessons. For example, if you are not an excellent communicator, you would want to reduce the amount of whole-group lecture and build more small-group and individualized activities for the students to complete as a delivery method.

You might want to ensure your style includes some humor at sparing times to ensure the jokes are extremely relevant with the content and hit with the audience a bit deeper, because they will not be expecting it. Your style might be one of empathy and sincerity, to which you are comforting in your approach, because you can show people how much you care without having to tell them.

Alternatively, you may not be as strong of a communicator, which may lead to less transparency about yourself and keeping the content strictly business and real-world applications. However, you may include one small detail about yourself to show a slight human side to your audience.

Lastly, you might pick a modality where you are more virtual and may conduct more asynchronous lessons, because being on camera all the time might be physically, mentally, and emotionally exhausting.

We will discuss more strategies as we explore further the "C's" that lie ahead. The main concept behind the next two chapters is NOT that you must completely change who you are. It is about finding your values as an educator and recognizing what you are missing, then making slight adjustments to get you out of the comfort zone to grow those weaknesses into neutral or even positive components.

Exploring Requires Documentation

The next three chapters on the first three "C's" – *command, change,* and *confidence* - is all about self-exploration, which means you need to monitor your progress diligently along the way. If you do not fully explore and detail certain occasions where you had small victories or misses, you are not going to recognize the changes on your course that might be necessary. Remember, growth is difficult, but necessary.

Pay close attention to documentation including student feedback, evaluations, and critiques from those above you and on the same path you are. Get as much resounding evidence as possible because it will help you to shape yourself, like the amoeba we will discuss in the next few chapters. Don't worry; I will definitely explain!

This type of documentation requires you to be "in the moment" as much as possible and reflect after each period, session, or block of teaching time. It requires metacognition, which basically means thinking about the way you think. Jot a few notes down, keep an active productivity journal, or document key findings digitally on the computer. Even if you write your findings on a sticky note or nine, perfect. Just get the information down! The best explorers write captain's logs, journal entries, or additional notes to ensure they do not fall into the same traps the next time they explore.

Once you have journaled for a week, take some time to block off key patterns that have occurred. Did you notice that you got five laughs this week on content related to customer service? Mark it as a must keep. Didn't get the serious feedback you were looking for during a heartfelt share of content on better writing practices? Make a shift and try something new. The point is to write, read, reflect, and adjust where necessary.

This type of reflection is crucial to an elite educator's success because it causes the educator to always be on your toes, and it requires a certain amount of thick skin to toughen you up. Without this type of reflection, the common phrase of "this is just how I am" begins to develop, followed by complaints about other people or students, then the worst of all, burnout and attrition.

Avoid falling into traps during your documentation process like not writing down things that may hurt your feelings or choosing not to reflect on a certain piece because it may have been a good week. Allow everything to be processed. This will make you a much strong educator in the end.

It's All About Growth and Balance

The best growth that can occur is in times of adversity AND in times of triumph. Most people will tell you that failure is the greatest teacher of all. Success is an amazing teacher as well. It is imperative to write and reflect on the victories and the plights during this voyage and find stability in the process. For your victories, reward yourself and make it a part of who you are. For your downfalls, wipe the dirt off and make the necessary adjustments. This type of growth is about what is in front of you and moving forward with the information you have. Reflect on the past and build the future.

An important note to consider is this: Whatever you do, do not blame others for any issues that have occurred. It is so easy to fall into the trap of saying "This lesson didn't work with this group because they did x" or "The online platform worked really slowly so that's why they didn't enjoy the class." How about my favorite: "They just weren't engaged with what I had to say because they weren't paying attention." If you have one or two students on occasion who are not into your lessons, then you can definitely say that is the case. If an entire class goes is not engaged, you must look within and truly reflect on why it didn't work. Blaming the choppy waters or storms is not something we can control. More on that in the next chapter...

At the same time, do not beat yourself up over it! I have seen the flip side of educators saying, "Maybe this isn't cut out for me" or "I just don't think I can connect with my students." This is not the approach either. Poking holes in your ship is not going to have you go very far on your voyage. Understand that you are not perfect. Allow yourself to find the equilibrium in the positivity of your victories and the growth points in your flaws. Simply put: Balance is everything.

Now that you have taken care of your ship, have left the dock, and see the open waters ahead, we are ready for the voyage on the first "C," which is all about *Command* of your ship. If you have made it this far, I honestly believe you will love the experience that is ahead of your teaching journey.

CHAPTER 3:
THE FIRST "C" - COMMAND

The clock says 8:30 AM and you arrive early to set up for an onsite teaching event that begins at 9:00 AM. Although you have double-checked your presentation several times the night before and early this morning, you just realized that Microsoft PowerPoint needs an important update to work in Slide Show mode. On top of that, your students are just starting to enter the classroom (even though they were told 8:45 AM) and you must introduce yourself to ensure that you are starting off on the right foot before the session begins. What do you do? (Just so you know, this has happened on more than one occasion).

When you have amazing *command*, you can do both. In this case, it is important to be calmly transparent about the Microsoft PowerPoint update that needs to occur. And while the PowerPoint is uploading, you take a few minutes to get to know the students that entered your class. Ask them about the traffic, the weather, their favorite sports teams, their hobbies, or anything you can find to keep the wheel steady while you are updating your computer. Inform the students that your computer needs to have a quick update and it should be a moment for the presentation to appear on the big screen.

Speaking of which, make sure the projector is off so that the students do not see you fumbling around to reopen the presentation. Ensure that other technology is working appropriately and make sure that your contact is aware of the situation as well. Finally, once the computer restarts, get your presentation into Slide Show mode, turn on the projector, and make sure you have everything else in order, while still sharing information and engaging with the students about your experiences.

You got all that? If not, that is perfectly okay, because this is what *command* is all about and it takes a ton of practice and situational understanding to apply appropriately.

Command is about having the know-how to take control of your ship at every moment, regardless of the elements that are thrown in your way. It is about being able to know and rely on your strengths so that you can tackle every obstacle in your way without fail. Most importantly, *command* is about knowing when and how to *stay the course.*

One of the hardest parts about knowing how and when to stay the course is that it is extremely tough to control the wheel if you do not know how to drive. You cannot manage situations and stay the course if you do not know how to manage yourself in those situations. It takes focus, self-awareness, situational awareness, and adept problem-solving to conquer these issues. Plus, keeping a level head will do you wonders because the last thing you want to do is show your audience you do not have control of yourself in tough situations.

It is incredibly easy to command the wheel and rely on your strengths when the waters are smooth. All you must do is showcase that you know how to keep a wheel straight and ensure your values come through your lesson. When you have issues with the content or audience, however, knowing yourself and how you will approach the situation takes a ton of knowledge, skill, composure, and belief.

Once again, anyone can be a decent educator if they know their content inside and out. It is what allows the students to believe that you are a credible source of information. It is important that your content has substance, meaning behind the information, examples that can be digested by your audience and real-world application knowledge with this information presented.

What separates the elite educators from the decent ones is the ability to *command* the room with your presence using strengths you possess. It is about knowing how to deliver the content in a way that truly resonates and impacts the audiences' viewpoints and perspectives, all while juggling several hats with technology, content, and platforms.

The *command* of your ship should work like the bolts that hold your wheel together, so that it stays grounded. They should be firmly secure and in place, but still allow you to spin and change direction as needed.

Tying to CYA and the Four Components of Yourself

As I mentioned in the last chapter, we are going to view the best approaches associated with the four components of the CYA Model of Preparation, but this is about knowing yourself in how you showcase your *delivery*, *style*, *transparency*, and *modality*. The purpose of *command* and these four components allows you to identify and build on your current strengths in the way you present and deliver information to others. Evaluating your strengths and knowing your control of each will allow you to ensure those bolts are firmly tightened, so that your core values always stay present in front of your students. Let's take a closer look at your strengths associated with each.

Let's review the *Teacher Mindset Statement (TMS)* again to gain further understanding of how this applies to *command*.

- **If I am/possess/have** _____ **(Strength), I would/should/ can** _____ **(Action that supports strength) into my educational lesson to ensure better** _____ **(Delivery/Style/ Transparency/Modality). This will make me a better educator because** _____ **(Reason that supports strength).**

Notice the approach used here: The word *strength* is listed three different times. That is because the only impactful thoughts for these TMS's should be strengths and values. The point here is *intense empowerment*. This will provide you with the belief, power, self-efficacy, and concentration to make sure your teaching is always in control and never wavers in the face of adversity. Without this empowerment, you will never have control of your ship.

A very important rule in teaching is this: You do not have to know 100% of the answers, but 100% of the answers you provide better be accurate and shared with the utmost control and confidence. Having and understanding your *command* through these TMS's provides you with stability, control, and potency in the way you share information with others.

I implore you: DO NOT focus on any weaknesses. We should only focus on the strengths and values that you know makes you a solid teacher and how it applies to each of the four components of The CYA Model of Preparation. If your strength can apply to all four components of *Yourself,* you will know when you have a core strength and know that you should use this as a key aspect in your *command* in teaching others. These core strengths are the anchors that hold you firm during the storm. It is imperative that we do not discuss any weaknesses here because it begins to generate self-doubt in the most important strengths you possess. Simply put: Do NOT be modest for these types of TMS's!

Command of Delivery

Understanding the *command* of your delivery allows you to recognize where you can truly drive the most important points home with your audience. Remember that delivery is a method of engagement and providing information to your students, as in being able to approach learning methods in multiple ways. This includes using cooperative learning, question and answer, whole-group lecture, inquiry-based learning, hands-on learning, or small group breakouts.

Knowing which one of these approaches you have true *command* over will help you to gain confidence in your approach and becomes your biggest asset in the type of educator you currently are. This self-assessment of understanding provides a firm stance on the tactics you can employ to teach students in the most effective way possible.

Before we apply the TMS to your teaching delivery, it is important to ask yourself three questions about the way you deliver a lesson to your students. Answer these questions as honestly as possible:

1. **What is your favorite part of teaching in the classroom setting? What about teaching in the online setting?**

2. **Do you prefer to have the students take charge of an assignment, or do you prefer to lead them through it? Why?**

3. **Which parts of your answers lead to successful results in your lesson delivery? How can you tell?**

Once you have answered those three questions honestly, it is time to think a bit deeper. For the first question, did you say it was presence or being in control of their attention? Did you say that it is when you are circulating the room during activities? Did you say when you are having a direct conversation with them and asking them questions? Each of these answers lead to a particular strength.

For example, if you said it is the control of their attention, you are most likely a fantastic orator and engager. If you said circulating during activities, then you are most likely a great delegator and can find individual strengths in teams. If you said direct conversation, you are amazing at interpersonal communication and inquiry-based learning.

For the second question, it is important to recognize whether your delivery strategy is a student-based classroom or a leader-led classroom. If you let your students take more control, you believe in a student-led classroom. If you have students focus on your guidance of the lesson, you believe in a leader-led classroom. Both are strengths, but it is important for you to recognize why each it important to utilize in your delivery.

The final question is essential to ask because it confirms your beliefs. If you enjoy delegating and creating team-based assignments and your students are missing the message in the lesson, then it is not really a strength. But if there is power behind this approach that you take, then it is absolutely a core strength that you should keep in your arsenal. It serves as a checkpoint that your delivery approach has success.

The purpose of asking these questions is to put your finger on the aspects of your delivery that are successful and to build lessons that incorporate those strengths. Now that we have our answers, it is time to apply them to your TMS for your strengths in Appendix A – Strengthening Teacher Mindset Statement Template.

When creating your TMS statements, do not think of these as four separate entities, but rather four pieces of the whole. In the center of your template, you would write down a key strength, for example – *Excellent Communication*. Then in the top-left corner of the template, you would write your S-TMS.

- *Example S-TMS for Delivery:* **If I am** *an excellent communicator,* **I would** *want to have more of a whole-group lecture, with question-and-answer sessions to directly focus on the students' individual questions to ensure more meaningful delivery and discussion in my class. Then I would shift into a hands-on or small group breakout to mix up my delivery approach.* **This will make me a better educator because I** *can ensure a passionate and enthusiastic delivery while providing a break from over-communicating with the group during the lessons taught.*

You will notice that your strength in delivery becomes your mission, which when practiced completely, becomes your mindset. That is why S-TMS are named what they are. The concept becomes your mindset with practice and constant implementation for each of the components in the *Yourself* section. Now that we have one down, let's move to *style* to see if the strength you have found can apply to the other next *Yourself* component of the CYA Model of Preparation.

Command of Style

Now that we have found a key strength based on our *delivery*, it is time to see if this is a strength that can also apply to our *style* of teaching. To recap from Chapter 1, *style* is the unique approach taken that allows you to be *you*, both as a teacher and as a person. This is where you get to decide the type of teacher or educator you are going to be. I used an example in the last chapter where the S-TMS was focused around having *dry humor* as a unique attribute of a teaching style.

For this approach, we need to ask three more questions that associate more with your authentic personality. Once again, answer these questions as honestly as possible:

1. **What is the best aspect of your personality that your students genuinely appreciate about you?**

2. **Does this personality trait embody who you are as a person?**

3. **Which parts of your answers lead to successful results in your teaching style? How can you verify this?**

Once you have answered those three questions honestly, let's deep-dive again. For the first question, you are locating a quality that your students truly appreciate, not just as a teacher, but as a person. The second question centers around whether this personality trait is an attribute that you use in your classroom technique only, or if it is a value that is truly engrained into who you are as a person. Remember that authenticity goes a long way with students, so if you can find a personality trait that also appeals to your students, then it will make a larger impact on their engagement and learning.

Once again, the final question is pivotal to ask because it confirms your beliefs. You will notice a pattern here because it is verifying that what you feel is also what you observe from others. If you are doing this honestly, then you are going to recognize the strength is universal and can be applied effectively.

This time, in the same template (Appendix A), you are going to write the S-TMS in the top-right corner for the *style* box. For example, let's say that *Excellent Communication* is an attribute that is a strength for your *style* of teaching:

- *Example S-TMS for Style:* If I am **an excellent communicator,** I would **want my teaching style to allow my lessons to involve speaking a bit more and include theatrics** to ensure better **higher engagement and more fun during the lesson**. This will make me a better educator because I **can be able to capture attention and explicitly share information to others in a way that will be exciting**.

My style will include theatrics, consisting of humorous jokes at appropriate times to lighten up the content. Then I will shift to more of a serious nature to drive my most important points home.

If you are beginning to see a pattern that the listed strength aligns to both your *delivery* and your *style*, you are heading on the right path toward having a core strength in your *command*! With two components aligned, the likelihood that this strength in knowing Yourself is going to apply to the other two components is very high. Just in case, let's move to the next *Yourself* component – *Transparency*, to see if the strength you have found can also apply.

Command of Transparency

The *Command of Transparency* is a very difficult one in which to find a strength because it requires the highest level of honesty. After all, *transparency* is about honesty. It is about deciding how genuine and open you are going to be with your audience. This is about deciding what to share in the moment and more importantly, what not to share.

The beginning of this chapter explains the importance of being able to think and speak on the fly about the information in front of you. The example showcased a situation where the computer needed an update, and the PowerPoint Slide Show was not working. Many educators and teachers would essentially hide this information because A) they do not want to get off on the wrong foot, B) they do not want to seem as if they were unprepared, and C) they do not want to essentially worry the students by not getting started on time.

This is where true *transparency* comes into play. In this situation, if you feel you have it under control, it is perfectly okay to calmly (and maybe even jovially) explain that technology needed an update. Go figure! Using an open, transparent explanation while still displaying your calm and collected demeanor can win double points.

That is what makes *transparency* so difficult, yet so powerful. It requires you to decide what insights you are going to share openly with your audience to build better trust and relationships. It also requires you to not be completely open and honest with the students. If someone asks a question and you say, "I actually do not know that answer," that might be okay. However, saying that you know very little about the subject matter might be TOO transparent. It is imperative you read the situations carefully and share the information that is going to provide a mutual benefit and understanding in the process.

Lastly, *command of transparency* is about divulging vulnerable attributes about yourself that you might not have originally considered because of the deeper level of connection that can be built from it. In training or teaching, I always share information about my family. You see, I have four daughters. Two are biological and two are adopted. They are in all different walks of life (high school graduate, 4th grader, preschooler, toddler), and I love watching them grow up to be wonderful young ladies.

I like to share this information with my students for a couple of reasons. First, I share because it is a unique thing about me that some members of the audience can relate to and others can appreciate. A second reason is that this becomes a conversation starter to quickly engage the audience into liking me as a person immediately.

Now, I must stress this: Do not divulge personal information simply for a manipulation reason! If they believe that you are only sharing to gain brownie points, you are done before you even begin. When I share this information, I do it because my family is extremely important to me and anyone who has children can understand the bond between a parent and child. The fact that it may provide me with some likability is not why I adopted and had a total of four children. But it does help if I show some *transparency* in my life with the audience because I become more relatable to them. Once again, the key words that I must stress is to be *authentic* and *real*. If you are going to be *transparent,* you must have the absolute *command* of the information you are sharing and know your purpose for sharing it.

To decide whether your strength is an important component of *transparency*, you must ask the following four questions:

1. **What information do I share openly with my audience?**

2. **Why do I choose to share this information with them?**

3. **Does this information sharing provide a benefit in the way that I connect with them? If so, how?**

4. **Which parts of your answers demonstrate how your *transparency* impacts the students in a positive way for the rest of your lesson?**

Let's go with our strength of being an excellent communicator. If you are an excellent communicator, how does that help with the classroom environment you want to build? Do you want to showcase transparency in this way? If you answered the questions honestly, you will have found an important answer to help you complete yourself. For this example, I have provided an S-TMS, which will be written in the bottom-left corner of the same template in Appendix A:

- *Example S-TMS for Transparency:* **If I am *an excellent communicator*, I would *want my students to know more personal information about me. I would want to generate a classroom environment that promotes more transparency and openness with my students* to** ensure better *open-mindedness and creativity in our discussions.* **This will make me a better educator** *because I can communicate in a way that does not overshare too much personal information, while still letting students feel like they are invested in a part of my life.*

Now we have three different components that truly demonstrate that being an excellent communicator is a strength and can be applied to daily practices in your instruction. As you can see, because of your excellent communication skills, you would absolutely have *command* over teaching in leader-led instruction with engaging, humorous lecture, and still be able to showcase honesty and openness with the audience to draw their attention. We are almost there! Now, we just need to see if this strength can tie closely with the component of *modality*.

Command of Modality

The *Command of Modality* is the final bolt that holds the wheel firmly in its place and keeps your ship staying the course. It is the final aspect of *yourself.* It is about knowing every "nook and cranny" of the environment you are entering: Online vs. F2F, the type of platform, various pods and panels, additional features you can utilize to engage your audience, audio checks, and physical environments. It means you are able to possess complete control over the environment in which you are teaching, and even when you don't have control, you have control over what to do next.

Think about every aspect that goes into *modality.* It is incredibly vast and extremely unyielding. As much as I know that change is inevitable, I know that technology is a massive blessing and a curse. It has made our lives so much easier, but it has placed us completely dependent as well. What happens when the modality we are teaching in does not work the way we want it? Even worse: What happens when it doesn't work at all.

This is where knowing yourself and your strengths are even more crucial. When you are teaching in many different formats, you must know how to steer the ship in each format. With *modality*, you are facing a storm to which you have no idea which direction it is blowing. Knowing your best attributes to help you maneuver through the waters will help you get through the storm much easier. But how?

By preparing and getting to know how you can properly shine on the platform or in the environment you are teaching. Remember, the *modality* is not supposed to lead you; you are supposed to use the *modality* to lead others.

I used an example earlier about PowerPoint needing an update and a restart, and the students were walking in the door. It is one thing to be honest about the situation. It is another to know the steps you need to take while still maintaining a calm demeanor. Can you inform your audience that PowerPoint needs an update and a restart, but that you have it all under control and still pay close attention to them? If you can rely on your strength in the way you know the *modality* you are teaching, you absolutely can do it. Here are four final questions to help:

1. **What modality am I using to teach? F2F? Online?**
2. **What are attributes of the modality that I can use to my advantage and build a better rapport with my audience?**
3. **What are some strategies I can use to better showcase the power of the modality while still showcasing my teaching as well?**
4. **Which parts of your answers demonstrate that how you teach positively impacts the teaching environment?**

Let's finish with our strength of being an excellent communicator. If you are an excellent communicator, how does that help with the *modality* you are encountering? How does your strength enhance the *modality* that is being used? Are you in front of a crowd? Be the actor. Are you in front of a webcam? Be the YouTuber. Are you training over a telephone conversation? Be the voice of reason. By knowing your strengths associated with each *modality* you come across, you know where you can make the largest impact.

If you answered the questions honestly, you will have found the final piece to your strength puzzle, which will complete the strength in the *Yourself* component. One last time, I have provided an S-TMS, which will be written in the bottom-right corner of the same template in Appendix A:

- *Example S-TMS for Modality:* **If I am *an excellent communicator*, I would *want to ensure that the modality I use is either Face-to-Face or includes a camera* to ensure better *body language and expressions in my teaching approach*. This makes me a better educator *because I can fully show my communication skills to my audience in a way that is suitable to my personality*. If I must teach in a different modality, like a phone call or in a web-conference without cameras, then I must ensure that my tone, pitch, and pace are equally as excitable.**

Notice an important description here follows around a sense of preparation. You are not only recognizing how your strength can lead in the whole area of *modality*, but how you can shine in each *modality* you teach. It is imperative that you study the *modality* holistically but know how *you* can use it to gain a better grasp of their attention and engagement.

How will you know? Listen to the feedback. Many people are afraid of learning online, but when you get comments that say, "I was expecting to just sit back but she was incredibly engaging!" Or better yet: "In the x number of years I have done training, I would never have thought that my best experience would be an online one!" These comments will truly show you that you have complete *command* over the *modality* you are working with.

Commanding the Ship

Whew! We navigated the first "C" and showed incredible *command* of our strength. Now, the idea is to build a few more TMS statements to really ensure that you have complete control over yourself and the way you teach. It takes true reflection for you to know what you do well in the physical and virtual classroom.

One of the biggest questions I normally receive is knowing how many strengths you need to truly have *command*. The answer is as many as you feel you need to have complete control. My personal advice behind commanding your ship is making sure that you have at least three to four core strengths to rely on. Using Appendix A, this means you should have about twelve to sixteen S-TMS's to build within your classroom environment. If you need even more strengths, then go for it!

For example, I have found that my S-TMS's for *myself* revolve around unwavering positivity, authentic enthusiasm, a burning desire to lead, and individualized connection with the audience. There are at least twelve total S-TMS's that can support it, and I know I can rely on them no matter what content I teach. That is how I truly know *myself* as a teacher. This is how I absolutely know that I have complete *command* of my ship. Do you have the same confidence every day in utilizing your strengths? If not, that is what the third "C" (*Confidence*) is for.

You will know when you have a true core strength that makes you an amazing teacher because it applies to all four components of *Yourself* and you know how and when to utilize them in certain teaching situations. This takes practice, diligence, patience, and speed. Once you have it mastered, however, you will see the power that you have over the audience and the command of yourself in the process.

Now that your ship has its bolts tightened and you have recognized some strengths that make you an incredible educator, it is time to start putting these to practice!

CHAPTER 4:
THE SECOND "C" - CHANGE

Now that you have fully acquired and owned your strengths, it is time to move further inward on this journey and recognize the most important changes we need to make. This is an intense journey because it requires us to encounter the biggest storms and decide how we approach and adjust accordingly.

As important as knowing your strengths and values is in your teaching methods, it is equally important to understand and embrace change to improve your weaknesses. The first "C" is about owning what makes you a strong educator. This second "C" takes you to the next level toward mastery in your craft.

Everyone recognizes that change is needed, but why don't more amazing educators exist? Because they do not make the extra tangible efforts to create and live that change. They understand but do not embrace change. They admit but do not seek a new way of delivery.

This is what the second "C" is about: Knowing not only when to stay the course but also when to adjust your course into a direction that will allow you to go further in your voyage. The question is: How amazing do you want to be as an educator?

If the answer to your question is *good* or *solid*, you do not need to read much further. The first "C" alone should have you know your strengths well enough to be a good educator who is comfortable with their approaches.

If you are looking for *amazing* or *outstanding* teaching, then continue the voyage ahead with the second "C." You will find the waters choppy, but you will also learn how to navigate your own practices much more effectively and truly gain a deeper appreciation for your teaching.

If you are excited and curious to find out how, I am going to introduce you to the three "R's" behind the ideals of *change*. Brace yourself for impact!

Three Major Ideals of Change

Change as an educator is about three major ideals: Recognition, Readjustment, and Reform. These three ideals ensure that you avoid denial and own your weaknesses, practice when situations arise with those weaknesses, and make these changes a part of daily routine until they become second nature.

First, without a recognition of change, you ship will consistently be moving against the current and will not take you as far as you would like to go. This is normally the easiest of the three ideals to achieve because most educators admit they are not perfect. The difficulty in this area however is taking more time and effort to fully understand *why* they are not perfect. It causes us to open wounds in our teaching practices that we have protected and avoided for years.

I will provide a brutally honest example. I have struggled for years with building effective activities because I thrived at direct lecture in an engaging fashion. It was a tough pill to swallow because this seemed to be the consensus of my biggest weakness. For the first few years of my teaching, I avoided activities altogether like they were shark-infested waters. This was until the evaluations keep attacking my ship and shaking my confidence.

One evaluation read "Jay was incredibly passionate about the content, but I wish there would have been more activities to enhance the learning." Another stated "The activities were okay, but it would have been nice if they were tied more closely to what we were learning." This one hurt: "The activities did not really tie to the real-world application I was looking for." Ouch. Ego down.

Now, I could have simply said "You know what? My final scores are still fairly high, and they seemed to like my passion, enthusiasm, and question and answers sessions a lot, so I am doing good enough." That would be staying comfortable with the first "C" and never moving forward toward great education. Instead, I fully recognized the impact of my lackluster activities and readjusted my course.

If you are asking yourself about ways to gather or understand your weaknesses, there are a few ways I suggest:

- Gather anonymous 360 feedback from your students or clients

- Assemble a brief "firing squad" session with your students and be openly honest that you want to change your practices and need their help.

- Seek observations from a peer, fellow instructor, or a manager/principal to have them provide honest feedback for you.

- Be brutally honest with what you don't like about your teaching approach and look inward to find exactly what it is that is holding you back (See Appendix B, which we will discuss in this chapter).

Regardless of the method you use, there is only one belief I suggest: Be 100% honest with yourself in the recognition. Without that honest recognition, you will never be able to move to the next step: Readjustment.

Once you have braved the honesty within yourself to recognize important change, the next step is to forcefully act and shake it up. Do your research, find applicable approaches that can associate to the way you teach, locate solid resources, ask those people not only for feedback but for advice. Whatever you do, do something.

Be valiant about your efforts, be potent with your embrace of change, and be convincing when you re-evaluate. The readjustment is the most important part because this is the part of the change that requires you to repeatedly make efforts to make yourself better. Just like lifting weights, eating healthier, typing more words per minute, or playing an instrument or a sport, it all requires practice. This is a conscious effort and cannot be taken haphazardly. *You must want to change.*

From here, the more you practice your readjustments and consistently make changes until you have mastered it, the more likely that Reform will occur. The reforming of your practice is where it becomes habit. You gain so much self-efficacy in the changes you made that you could trust it in every situation. More on that in the third "C," which is *confidence.*

Much like the first "C," this is where the Teacher Mindset Statement (TMS) comes back into play. The only difference is, we are trying to adjust so we need to have a Changing Teacher Mindset Statement, or C-TMS for this one. Let's bring back the four components of the CYA Model of Preparation, focusing on *Yourself* in how you showcase your *delivery, style, transparency,* and *modality.* The purpose of *change* and these four components allows you to recognize, readjust, and reform your practices that require major modifications. The C-TMS is more focused on making actionable changes to ensure better educational delivery, style, transparency, and modality adjustments.

- **If I do not possess/have** _____ *(Strength),* **I would/should/can** _____ *(Action that engages change)* **into my educational lesson to ensure better** _____ *(Delivery/Style/Transparency/Modality).* **This will make me a better educator because** _____ *(Reason that supports strength).*

It is valuable to make sure that you are as brutally honest with yourself as possible for this. At the same time, do not exaggerate your weakness to make it seem worse than it really is. Pay attention to feedback and try to be objective with this critique, as if you were observing someone else honestly to help them be better at their craft.

One of the key advantages with understanding the changes needed is that you can potentially tie them to a strength you have and make the change easier to implement. For example, if you are an excellent communicator but struggle with creating meaningful activities, it would be easier to build activities that involve speaking or acting. This ensures that if the change you need to make feels impossible, you have the S-TMS to review and attach the C-TMS to it to make the change easier to implement.

This is exactly why you must master *command* before seeking *change*. With that said, we are going to take a closer look at the changes you would want to define with *delivery*, *style*, *transparency*, and *modality*.

Change in Delivery

Embracing the changes required in your *delivery* means that you can sharpen the points of engagement you truly need. Remember that *delivery* is a method of engagement and supplying meaningful information in a way that students can connect and absorb. Just to remind you, this means using cooperative learning, question and answer, whole-group lecture, inquiry-based learning, hands-on learning, or small group breakouts.

This goes back to the example I used earlier in the chapter where my strength in *Command* existed in a whole-group lecture and inquiry-based learning, but my ability to create better hands-on learning and small group breakouts was limited. I had to assess myself to fixate and diligently work on this area to be more versatile and even more engaging from start to finish with every lesson I taught.

For you, it requires you to take a closer look at the parts of your delivery you feel need work. This becomes the lighthouse for your ship to make it ashore safely; it directs you when the storm is in your face.

Much like the previous chapter, it is important to ask yourself the questions below about the way you deliver a lesson to your students that identify how change. Answer these questions as honestly as possible:

1. **What is your *least* favorite part of standing in front of others in the classroom setting?**

2. **Do you prefer to have the students take charge of an assignment, or do you prefer to lead them through it? Why did you not choose the other?**

3. **Which parts of your answers do leave engagement gaps and disconnect between you and your students? How can you tell?**

Once you have answered those three questions honestly, it is time to think a bit deeper about why you feel that way. For example, if you said your least favorite part was delivering direct lecture to students in front of the classroom, it might mean you need to work on more showmanship in your teaching approaches. If you said circulating during activities is your least favorite, then you need to work on better delegation and proximity techniques during class. If you said asking the students questions because you don't like silence, then allow yourself the uncomfortable silence until they answer.

For the second question, it is important to understand why you did not choose the control aspect of your classroom. If you chose to take charge, why did you not like to have students in control? If you chose for the students to take charge, why do you not prefer to be in charge during delivery? This is important because it allows you to gain versatility and be able to switch more comfortably.

The final question must be asked. This is where the 360 feedback, survey evaluations, meetings with your managers/principals, and other comments shape you to adjust your practice. If you think you have great presence in front of your students, and they tell you that they wish you engaged more and brought more humor or passion in the classroom, there is a disconnect that requires readjustment. This is where the C-TMS statements come in. Go ahead and apply these ideas to your TMS for your changes needed using Changing - Teacher Mindset Statement Template (C-TMS) in Appendix B.

Just to remind you, do not think of these as four separate entities, but rather four pieces of the whole. In the center of your template, you would write down a key weakness, for example – *Weak with Creating Meaningful Activities*. Then in the top-left corner of the template, you would write your C-TMS.

- *Example C-TMS for Delivery:* **If I am *weak with creating meaningful activities*, I would *want to research more engaging activities that*** *tie directly to the content taught. Next, I would practice this activity aloud by myself to identify any final gaps. When class began, I would shift start the day's lesson with a small group breakout to mix up my delivery approach and show them power in my delegation skills.* **This will make me a better educator because I** *can ensure that the activities will create more meaningful depth in the content being taught and still engage them through active participation.*

You will notice that changes in delivery is the singular focus, which first becomes recognition, then becomes action and practice. The concept becomes the mindset with practice and constant implementation for each of the components in the *Yourself* section.

Also, you notice that if your strength is being an excellent communicator, engagement is something you can tie more creative and meaningful activities to, because it is familiar and reliable. Now that we have one component of change down, let's move to *style* to see if the changes for better activity creation can apply to the next *Yourself* component of the CYA Model of Preparation.

Change in Style

Now that we have recognized an area of growth and change for our *delivery*, it is time to see if this can be applied to our *style* of teaching. *Style* is the approach taken that allows you to be *you*, both as a teacher and as a person.

For this approach, we need to ask a few more questions that associate more with your authentic personality. Once again, answer these questions as honestly as possible:

1. **What is an aspect of your personality that you may be afraid of trying in your teaching style?**

2. **What disconnect exists between who you are as a teacher and who you are as a person?**

3. **Which parts of your answers have not led to results in your teaching style? How can you verify this?**

Once you have answered those questions honestly, let's deep-dive again. For the first question, you are locating a fear that stops you from being effective, not just as a teacher, but as a person. The second question centers around if a disconnect stops your personality from shining through as a teacher. If your personality is inhibited by a component of your teaching style and you feel that it stops you from being able to more closely connect with your audience, then it will ultimately leave a negative impact on their engagement and learning.

Once again, the final question is incredibly essential to ask because it confirms your beliefs. You will notice a pattern here because it is verifying that what you feel is also what you observe from others. If you are doing this honestly, then you are going to recognize the concern you have is universal and requires readjustment.

This time, in the same template (Appendix B), you are going to write the C-TMS in the top-right corner for the *style* box. For example, let's say that *Creating Meaningful Activities* is a weakness for your *style* of teaching:

- *Example C-TMS for Style:* **If I am *weak with Creating Meaningful Activities*, I would *want my activities to better reflect my personality for my students* to ensure better *higher engagement and more individuality during the lesson. I would want to better use theatrics to better engage them in participation as this is a style that reflects my personality and can still allow them to shine.* This will make me a better educator because I *can show through activities that my personality can be better applied through activities and does not solely rely on me to supply theatrics in an educational setting.***

If you are beginning to see a pattern that the listed weakness aligns to both your *delivery* and your *style*, you are heading on the right path toward seeking change. Notice that with the C-TMS's, you not only have recognition of your weakness, you have a path and can begin to see how to apply certain changes to mix with your *command* of your strengths from the previous chapter. If you are an excellent communicator, but struggle with creating meaningful activities, you can build activities that revolve around communication and individuality.

Once again, if you have two components of change aligned between *delivery* and *style*, the likelihood that this is a dedicated change for the other two components is very high. Just in case, we will shift to the next *Yourself* component – *Transparency*, to see if the C-TMS can be tied to your S-TMS here and determine what changes might be necessary.

Change in Transparency

If the *Change in Transparency* is about deciding how genuine and open you are going to be with your audience, then it is truly essential for you to be as raw and open with yourself as possible. Determining how honest you are going to be with your audience about your weakness is a critical element to decide. Knowing what not to share is equally as valuable as knowing what to share, and in this case, reading your audience to determine what they value is critical.

For the example used here, having a weakness in creating meaningful activities is a tricky situation to decide if you share this with your students. It is extremely important to share that you are trying new things, but it is equally important to not share that you are weak with creating activities. Again, displaying your calm and collected demeanor is crucial while still being open to students.

How do we approach this? In this situation, if you try a new activity for the first time, you might decide to be honest with your students and say, "I am trying something different to make this activity as meaningful as possible." You might say "Alright, one thing I am working on is building more meaningful activities, so let me know what you think!" Sharing that you are working on growth is always a best practice, as long as you know what your strengths are.

Remember this point: Do not openly share that you are *weak* in a particular area. That is for you to keep for yourself to work on. Make the area of weakness appear as if you are making positive changes to enhance your teaching practice. After all, that is what you are doing. Sometimes we are too transparent to the point that we expose our weaknesses, and it causes doubt in the minds of your audience. Your goal is to show credibility, but what many do not know is that you can show even more credibility when you mention that you are growing as an educator as well in very specific areas.

To decide whether this *change* is an important component of *transparency*, you must ask the following three questions:

1. **How to I demonstrate to my audience that I am growing in this area?**

2. **Does the shared information provide a benefit in the way that I connect with them? If so, how?**

3. **Do I ask them for feedback on the activity? If so, what specifically am I looking for?**

Let's go back to our example of weakness that we need to work on *creating meaningful activities*. If you feel that you are weak in this area, how do you showcase that you are growing? If you answered the questions honestly, you will have found an important answer to help you complete yourself. I have provided a C-TMS, which will be written in the bottom-left corner of the same template in Appendix B:

- *Example C-TMS for Transparency:* If I am **weak at creating meaning- ful activities,** I would **want my students to see that I am showcasing a new activity that I would like their feedback on. Because I am an effective communicator, I would want to explain the intended meaning of the activity very diligently and ask for specific infor- mation about what they liked and did not like** to ensure better *open-mindedness and creativity in the way I adjust these activities for the future.* This will make me a better educator *because I can take the feedback and appropriately make changes to build more meaningful activities.*

Now we have three different components that tether your C-TMS to your S-TMS, you can gather the information needed to tangibly make changes and openly look for new ways to succeed. Once again, it is crucial to note that your ability to take a weakness and tie it to your strength will make it easier to *change* course as needed. Lastly, we need to determine how this weakness of creating meaningful activities would be affected in using a different *modality*.

Change in Modality

The *Change in Modality* is incredibly valuable because you not only need to recognize the *change* itself, you need to recognize how the change affects the environment you are teaching. Remember that if you are teaching in an Online vs. F2F environment, the change might even need to be greater. You will need to properly know how the additional features in an online platform can help you to better grow as an educator.

For example, if you are weak at creating meaningful activities and you teach in both an online live and a F2F environment, you must envision what that activity needs to look like in both. If you are putting the students into groups, F2F makes that easy because they are physically moving to a different section of the room. However, doing this in an online setting requires you to know how to properly use the breakout sessions in the platform, while still knowing how that activity is going to have a meaningful impact. It requires such a focal effort and a keen sense of awareness in how the activity is going to play out.

This is where knowing your strengths are even more crucial. If you are an excellent communicator, how are you going to communicate the directions of the activity in an online setting? Do you have the step-by-step capability to walk them through exactly how the activity is supposed to work? Do you have the expectations in advance? This weakness is the toughest in my opinion because you need to know how to adjust on an area where you already feel you are lacking. It takes much more work and much better preparation.

However, if you can rely on your strength in the way you know the *modality* you are teaching and you believe that you can make strong adjustments, you absolutely can do it. Here are a few final questions to help:

1. **What modality am I using to teach? F2F? Online?**

2. **What specific adjustments do I need to make in the different modality to which I am teaching?**

3. **What are attributes of the modality that I can use to my advantage when I am working on making changes for my weakness?**

Let's finish with our weakness of creating meaningful activities. How does the activity itself need to change with the *modality* that is being used? If you are physically in front of the crowd, what part of the activity will resonate the most with them? If you are in an online setting, what can you do with the breakout areas online to further enhance instructions and facilitate greater learning? If you are training over a telephone conversation, how can you virtually walk them through the activity to create better understanding and help them visualize the greater picture? In any *modality*, what are your major objectives to accomplish?

If you answered the questions honestly, you will have found the final piece to your strength puzzle, which will complete the strength in the *Yourself* component. One last time, I have provided a C-TMS, which will be written in the bottom-right corner of the same template in Appendix B:

- *Example C-TMS for Modality:* If I am **weak with creating meaningful activities**, I would **want to make sure that I can effectively build and communicate the expectations of the activity** to ensure the **breakout session works the same way online as it would be used** *in a F2F session.* This makes me a better educator *because it shows my students can fully participate and still gain the meaning and purpose of the activity created.*

Because *modality* can change, you must do extra planning and preparation here. You must go out on a limb and test it in an environment and walk through the activity effectively. The expectations must be crystal clear. If that is a major strength, the tether becomes even stronger because you can use the communication to shine in how you ensure the activity is effective.

You recognized your change! Although your strengths provide the foundation, your ability to recognize change is what elevates good instructors, teachers, professors, and educators to the next level. More importantly, you recognize that the change you need to make can be done much more easily if you have a strength you can connect it to.

Changing the Course of Action

We have weathered a very tough storm on this voyage! But in doing so, you are now able to better navigate your deepest fears and biggest weaknesses. This allows you to change the course of action and gain better experience when navigating the next change. Because you can use your strengths and weaknesses as tools for change, you can practice utilizing them in different educational situations and see what minor adjustments need to be made over time. This is essentially what gives you the validation you seek as an effective educator.

Again, it is not about having a certain number of changes you must make. It is about recognizing the weakness after every discussion, collaboration, meeting, activity, or lecture and having an intense willingness to make the changes necessary to ensure better success. My final piece of advice in this chapter is to recognize how your strengths can help you change your weaknesses. You can better navigate the choppy waters, ruthless storms, and the vast darkness when you have beacons of light showing you the way to help you change. Not to mention, it will help you gain a huge sense of accomplishment and confidence.

Once we have our strengths and changes intact and are ready to practice, it is time to start our final Voyage Inward with the third "C": The "C" of *confidence*!

CHAPTER 5:
THE THIRD "C" - CONFIDENCE

I have two quick questions for you: 1) Before you began this book, what was your confidence level to effectively educate others and create more meaning? 2) What is your confidence level now that you have sailed the first two "C's?"

If the confidence level was higher in the first question, you already have learned some effective techniques in the past but have probably come to the realization that the best teaching comes from within and there are things that require some real insight. This is beneficial because you have most likely gained a lot of valuable experience that has taught you to maneuver through difficult situations in teaching, and there is a recognition of deeper reflection in the way you make a deeper impact in your practices.

If the confidence level is higher in the second question, then you might not have started with a lot of confidence, and the first two "C's" have helped you find your balance a little bit. This is also excellent because it enables you to take cloudy information about your teaching practices and make things more visible in the way you approach.

Either way, understanding your existing confidence level in your teaching methods allows you to gain a sense of trust with yourself. You will be able to process the fact that you do a lot of great things in your teaching practices and still possess the ability to tangibly focus on the areas of growth that will propel you to the next level. There is nothing wrong with this. That is what confidence is all about: Locating your targets and firing with purpose.

The voyage of this "C" will not be as extensive as the previous two, but it is still incredibly valuable because it explores the steps needed to gain demonstrate conviction in your teaching beliefs and practices. *Confidence* is all about navigating the "C of Selfs."

Sound ominous? Don't panic. We will demonstrate that the "C of Selfs" directly associates with your confidence and discuss how they are applied to S-TMS and C-TMS statements to further enhance your teaching practices.

The "C of Selfs" – Gaining a Deeper Meaning of Confidence

When we talk about gaining more confidence in your teaching ability, many textbooks will tell you that it is all about practice. They are not wrong, but there is so much more to that. Think about playing darts, shooting a bow and arrow, or firing a weapon at a target. First, you must identify your target.

The first time you aim and fire at a target, your goal is to merely hit the target. Then you hit the outer edge. You are happy, but you know there is room for growth. Then, you must identify what gives you the ability to hit that target and what gaps you have. You work on your aim, your stance, you approach, and you practice diligently. Then you hit one of the middle rings and you are ecstatic. You are confident the next time you fire, but you know there are still readjustments to be made. You make the adjustments, and you are still not hitting the bullseye. Not once, not twice, but repeatedly. It takes time and it takes a conscious effort to readjust, but the more you practice, the more confidence you must hit the target every time.

The way confidence is achieved in teaching and training is by recognizing and consciously applying a similar approach. This is what the "C of Selfs" is about. It is about achieving different levels that allow you to get closer to your overall target and gain more efficacy and value in *Yourself* when you teach.

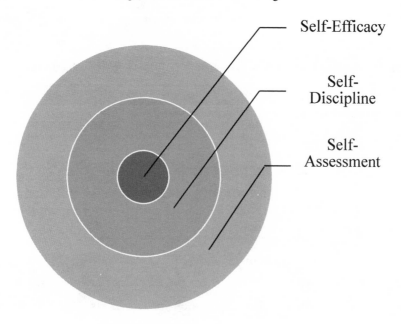

Figure 2: The "C of Selfs" Target

Self-Efficacy

Self-Discipline

Self-Assessment

The three different forms of self, as demonstrated in Figure 2, are *Self-Assessment*, *Self-Discipline*, and *Self-Efficacy*. The closer you get to the bull-seye, the more confident you are in your execution of your teaching practice every time. We are going to identify what each level means, why each level is important in helping you gain more confidence, and how you can employ each level in your selected *delivery*, *style*, *transparency*, and *modality*.

The Outer Ring: Self-Assessment

The outer ring of your teaching target is *self-assessment*. If you are assessing yourself with your *delivery*, *style*, *transparency*, and *modality*, then you are already hitting your target. The first two "C's" put you on that path, but the third "C" of confidence is about taking the shot and firing in your classroom teaching. It is about taking the shot and re-assessing consistently.

For example, if you recognize that you are a strong communicator but you lose that communication when you are working in small groups, assessing yourself to find out why is a critical step in helping you to gain your confidence. Performing self-assessments are incredibly important when shifting the inventory of your teaching practices.

Why is *Self-Assessment* so valuable? Because we fear the unknown. We fear change. We fear failure. Having a meaningful and reflective assessment of yourself provides clarity on all three of these fears, which in turn provides you with the desire and confidence to want to practice and give it another shot.

If you are asking yourself how you can better assess yourself with your teaching practices, first, look to your S-TMS and C-TMS diagrams. From there, you can also create surveys, interview students, discuss with fellow educators, or have a meeting with your leader or manager.

Whichever method you choose to assess yourself, *find the patterns.* Find the consistent information that appears throughout each. These are the first concerns that you practice. If your C-TMS indicates that you are struggling with being open about yourself with students, and your student surveys say that they don't feel like they get to know you very well, then working on your transparency is critical. If your C-TMS mentions that you are not very humorous, and a fellow teacher suggests bringing in more content relevant jokes, then work on your humor. The patterns will help you identify why your aim is off so that you can begin to practice.

Although you may feel like you are missing the target entirely, you are not. Therefore *Self-Assessment* is so valuable to the concept of *confidence.* The fact that you can identify patterns means you can shine a light on where changes need to be made. Remember: we fear what we do not know. Now you know, so there is nothing to fear.

The hard part is over, and you are actually on target now! Now, let's work on gaining more consistency and hitting the inner rings on the target.

The Middle Ring: Self-Discipline

The middle ring of the target is *Self-Discipline*. If you only assess yourself and do nothing with it, then you will live in negativity. Self-Discipline is about regulating your current practices and making active changes.

Having *Self-Discipline* does not only mean that you hold firm in your practices. If you are amazing with direct lecture for your students, then hold firm and keep that level of confidence! However, if your self-assessment patterns show that your delivery method of lecture is not as engaging as you thought it would be, decide on a change to make and stick to it! The students see that you tried something different, and even if you still only hit the outer ring, you can assess and retry.

Why is *Self-Discipline* so valuable? There are two reasons. First, it shows other people you are working on yourself to be a better educator and nearly everyone will appreciate that. There is something powerful about watching people try to grow and work hard to be better. Second, the more you practice on this skill, the more confidence you gain knowing what individual components are working well and which need minor adjustments.

What adjustments may be needed? For delivery, you might have tried a lesson with a goofy joke related to an Excel cell (Cell A1 = Steak Sauce), which might have been good, but you know it can be better. So you focus even deeper on a humorous joke and you go to cell C4 instead and make a wickedly animated explosion reference! The class giggles at how goofy you are, and you know you can do this moving forward. The next time, you incorporate another joke!

The adjustments are what make *Self-Discipline* so important. They are where you focus on the individualized aspects and make the minor changes that make the biggest difference. The more disciplined you are in making gives you the confidence to know that you can hit the mark more often. That's where the bullseye starts to become clearer.

It is equally as important to realize why you are not hitting your mark and staying tough when making the change. You must have the *Self-Discipline* to believe you can make this change and that the next change will be better. It requires an innate belief that you are going to solve the puzzle and you know how to push yourself to the next level.

The reason that *Self-Discipline* ties to *confidence* is clear: The more you practice a new skill, the more confident you feel to employ similar tactic next time. It also means you are more willing to try something new and take a leap of faith as well.

The question now becomes this: Do you want the confidence to be a *good* educator or a *great* educator? The next level requires you to have so much confidence that you know you can own the trait. Let's go for the bullseye!

The Bullseye: Self-Efficacy

The bullseye of the target is *Self-Efficacy*. The major concept behind this idea is mastery. Once you know you have your key components mastered for a particular area, you carry it naturally. It becomes a part of who you are.

Having *Self-Efficacy* means that you can deliver your lessons with the utmost confidence. We have seen these educators. They are amazing because they just ooze confidence in the way they share information with others. We want to be like them, but we never know how. Once you have self-assessed and you have practiced self-discipline in making the necessary changes, the efficacy to repeatedly deliver becomes cruise control for you.

Let's stay with the example of bringing humor into your lesson delivery. You have assessed that it is missing from your approach, and you have practiced bringing in humor to a few different lessons. You teach a lesson and it is a success! You now recognize that even though it was successful, there are still other pieces of humor you feel could have been incorporated. You attack! You get moving! You make the adjustments more quickly and you even smile when you are finished. You went from not having any humor, to maybe having too much humor, to recognizing and delivering the right amount in the right situations. This is *Self-Efficacy* in knowing yourself and having the *confidence* in yourself to master it.

This doesn't mean that the next arrow is going to hit the bullseye, but it does mean that you have the confidence to believe that every lesson you deliver is going to be the best lesson yet. It shows that even if a lesson hit a little off target, then you know the immediate steps you are going to take to *self-assess* and practice *self-discipline* to make it happen.

It also means that if you do not know something or do not feel confident in the response, you know you have enough mastery to pivot, make the adjustments on the fly, and get the answers necessary to help everyone thrive. That kind of *confidence* is rare, but it is powerful. And you can absolutely make it happen!

Confidence Applied to S-TMS's and C-TMS's

Many professionals would argue that it takes a lot of time and a lot of experience to master *self-efficacy*, but the truth is you can reach this level a bit sooner if you have the drive and determination to know your command and know what changes you need to make. That is the starting point, and many people take years to take a step back and find out what corrections they need to make in the *Yourself* phase. You are on your Voyage Inward already, so you are ahead of the game!

The place to start is the *command* chapter. This is where you focus on your strengths. This will show you what *Self-Efficacy* feels like and show you what mastery is supposed to be. You can review your S-TMS's and begin to assess others to see if the pattern is consistent. If it is, you know you got it down! If it is not, then maybe the S-TMS is not as strong as it could be. This means you know where you need to take *Self-Discipline* and begin to readjust.

Next, you want to review your C-TMS's to truly identify where you feel the gaps hold you back from being the educator you want to be. Once again, *self-assess* and assess others to see if the patterns match. If they do not, you might be too hard on yourself and the changes necessary might not be as bad as you think. If they are consistent, then you know where you really need to start working on your target.

A Final Note about The Voyage Inward: Build Your Acronym!

A final note for the first three "C's" in The Voyage Inward is a very important one. Understanding your *command*, *change*, and *confidence* is imperative, because you truly identify and have the efficacy to mold yourself into the teacher *you* want to be. Be yourself. But be an amazing version of yourself as an educator.

Once you have mastered the four components of *Yourself* (*delivery*, *style*, *transparency*, *modality*), create one final challenge for yourself before you dock your vessel for a break: Build your acronym.

Your acronym is your compass out on the sea. It is your reminder that you know who you are, even when all other doubts appear. You will know if you have achieved full mastery and efficacy when you can holistically define your *delivery* with the same four qualities that define you. Not only are you able to show it, but it also becomes who you are as an educator.

This is an incredibly arduous task and only happens when you have thoroughly reflected on The Voyage Inward. For example, what is one characteristic that you have mastered in *your delivery* that can be applied, regardless of delivery method. This means that the characteristic you have mastered can apply in direct lecture, small group, breakouts, cooperative learning, inquiry-based learning, and so on. The same applies that your *style* is applicable no matter what situation you are in, the *transparency* you show is consistent in every way, and that you can effectively teach in any *modality*.

I have spent a long time thinking about the educator I am, regardless of what types of students I was teaching. Whether they were 14-year-olds or senior executives, I made sure that these four qualities were attributes that I could rely on, no matter what. Once I have truly reflected on my Voyage Inward and sailed the first three "C's," I built the following acronym for myself. That acronym is PEAK. This stands for:

Table 3: Voyage Inward Acronym Example

P – Passionate – Regardless of who, what, where, or when I teach, I am a passionate educator in all situations.
E – Engaging – Regardless of the content, I am an engaging educator who can captivate an audience in all situations.
A – Authentic – Regardless of teaching environment, I am going to be authentic with every student in the virtual or physical space.
K – Kind-Hearted – No matter what, I am going to be kind and open about who I am and let my students into my life.

PEAK is the idea that if I am passionate about my craft, engaging with my audience, authentic with my connections with others, and kind-hearted in every interaction I encounter, then it is highly unlikely that I am going to fail as an educator.

This is my acronym. What will your acronym be? If you have fully taken advantage of The Voyage Inward, I bet it will be nothing short of amazing.

I hope that your voyage through the first three "C's" becomes one where you can truly reflect, gather, understand, find patterns, and work to find yourself as an educator. I will say that it has truly made a positive impact in my profession and in my life, and I hope that it has the same effect for you.

Now that you have mastered The Voyage Inward, it is time to take a small break, reward yourself, and get ready for the next voyage: The Voyage Outward!

CHAPTER 6:
THE VOYAGE OUTWARD

Whew! What an amazing voyage you were just on! So much self-reflection and so many shifts in mindsets. The question is: Are you ready for the next one?

If so, let's get into The Voyage Outward. The Voyage Outward focuses on the premise of how you make an impact on others in your teaching practices. It is about visualizing, reading, observing, connecting, discussing, opening, and seeking meaningful relationships during your lessons.

For those that argue that *Good teaching is good teaching*, I pose these two questions: Who deems what is good teaching? What qualifications make teaching good?

The problem is good teaching is always in the eye of the beholder and every eye beholds a different view. This is why The Voyage Outward is equally as valuable as The Voyage Inward. It requires you not only to understand what effective teaching is from your mindset, but from your audience's mindsets as well. Furthermore, it allows you to make connections between what you think your strengths are and what your audience finds your strengths to be.

When we hear of the best facilitators or educators, we hear phrases like *"I felt like he understood me,"* or *"She seemed to care about my success in a way that I didn't expect."* We hear these phrases and immediately tell ourselves that *this is who I want to be.* But we can't seem to put our finger on the pulse of how this is achieved. Until now.

The Voyage Outward aligns around three more "C's" that you will face: *Captivation* (Of Your Audience's Attention), *Clarity* (In Message and Meaning), and *Connection* (With Every Individual). This means you can engage, transmit energy, and engage your audience on a deeper level so that they can see, hear, and feel the presence you are bringing to every lesson.

The Voyage Outward is not as arduous as The Voyage Inward in terms of self-reflection and thinking about who you are as an educator. However, if not careful, you could think you are heading in the right direction with your teaching practices, and next thing you know, you are lost in the open waters.

How The Voyage Outward Works

The Voyage Outward is all about one word: *Transmission*. You will read this word a lot because it ensures that the principles you have set for yourself in the first three "C's" are being transmitted to your audience. It aligns the expectations that you have with yourself with the expectations that your audience has for you.

Let's revisit The CYA Model of Preparation to further explore how you become a masterful educator. Remember, the preparation of your content is normally achieved when you are learning to become an educator. You learn the importance of creating substance with your lesson, elaboration of your explanations, relevant examples to expand on the knowledge and real-world application to have them practice later. This is what allows you to become an educator, but it does not allow you to become a masterful educator.

With each of the "C's" on The Voyage Inward, we investigated the Yourself components in the CYA table. We discussed how you can find your *Command* and recognize needed *change* associated with your delivery, style, transparency, and modality. We also elaborated why *confidence* with the "C of Selfs" allows you to assess, practice, and gain efficacy to ensure you are the educator you want to be. Now that you have a firm grasp on the first eight components associated with your Content and Yourself, we are strictly going to focus on the Audience component with The Voyage Outward.

Table 4: The CYA Model of Preparation for the Voyage Outward

Content (Already Gained)	Yourself (Voyage Inward)	Audience (Voyage Outward)
Substance	*Delivery*	*Engagement*
Elaboration	*Style*	*Depth*
Relevant Examples	*Transparency*	*Alignment*
Real-World Application	*Modality*	*Trust*

The premise behind sailing these three "C's" on The Voyage Outward is to go in with a solid game plan to captivate and immediately engage your audience as a whole, ensuring that the message you deliver is one that is direct but purposeful. You should make sure you find opportunities to individually create a meaningful bond with every person in the room. If you can accomplish this in an entire unit, you will show you have power. If you can do this in one lesson, you will have achieved mastery in your craft.

There are three major differences between The Voyage Inward and The Voyage Outward:

1. The Voyage Outward focuses on *engagement, depth, alignment,* and *trust* because they emphasize the importance of *Transmission,* whereas The Voyage Outward takes the four components of *delivery, style, transparency,* and *modality* to emphasize the importance of *Identity.*

2. The guide for The Voyage Outward focuses on the way you are communicating with others when teaching, while helping you pay close attention to cues that you are or are not making a meaningful impact on your audience. It is going to require you to write and reflect with a "Captain's Log" of specific events that went particularly well, and a list of events that did not go well.

3. The Voyage Outward demonstrates how the prioritization of the four components begins to shift. This means that in Chapter 4, all

four components are discussed, but *engagement* will be the most important of the four. By Chapter 6, all four components are still discussed, but *trust* is the most important of the four.

Although these differences may seem somewhat intimidating in the shift in mindset, I want to inform you that I would never let you go on this journey without a map (or visual) that will help you assess and reflect on your current practices! I have provided two figures (Figure 3 and Figure 4), which show a difference in balance required between Chapter 7: *Captivation* and Chapter 9: *Connection*.

Figure 3: Importance of the Four Components of Audience

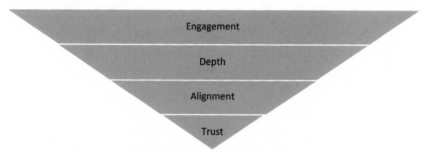

In Figure 3, you will see that *engagement* is located at the top of the triangle, and it is the broadest. *Engagement* is the foundation for captivating your audience. You are reaching the masses at once and making sure all members are engaged in what you are about to deliver. This will be discussed thoroughly in Chapter 7: *Captivation*.

Alignment and *depth* are important, but this will have a much greater impact when we reach Chapter 8: *Clarity*. Your goal with *clarity* is to start creating more significant and *clear* opportunities to build relationships with the audience. You must be *clear* that you are understanding their reasons for being a part of the experience. This allows you to begin to *connect* by building *trust*.

When you are connecting with your audience, you are relying on your ability to build *trust* to get them to show vulnerability, openness, and meaning. The greater emphasis requires you to build more meaningful trust.

Connection is also crucial to success because of its concentrated effort to create an impact with every individual in the room. If *engagement* is meant for the whole audience, *trust* is meant for every single person.

To build on each component, you must go through a few bumps and bruises in your preparation. First, this means that you are going to go through a lot of trial and error. Some things you try are going to be flat-out awful. Some things you try are going to be simply okay. Some things you try are going to be amazing. However, you must take a leap of faith and make a conscious effort to try.

This also means you are going to need to self-assess every time you try something new. You must document individual aspects that you particularly enjoyed and did not enjoy. Why did you enjoy it? Why wasn't it as good as you thought it would be? Once again, this voyage requires a sense of being brutally honest with yourself in the way you work with other people, so make sure the bolts in the wheel are securely fastened before setting sail!

Lastly, this means you are going to need to seek consistent and honest formative feedback from your audience as you try something new. You must set initial expectations and communicate that you are trying something new with a particular activity, lesson, idea, or joke. As it is occurring, observe! Be aware of verbal and non-verbal cues your audience is displaying. Are they laughing, smiling, or locked in with eye contact? Or are they dismissed or not engaged?

The best way to truly determine is to ask. If you ask them for honest feedback and to elaborate, you will gain the most direct insight toward your next steps in approaching your connection with them. Believe me, if you ask with honesty and confidence, they will be happy to share and will appreciate your efforts to grow.

Meet IROS: A Captain's Log

Wow. Seems like a lot, right? I would never leave you hanging on how to organize your thoughts! I have provided a table (Appendix C) that easily provides a way for you to log your perceptions of an idea you have attempted. Since I know how much you love acronyms, I have one more for you: IROS. IROS stands for Ideas, Reflections, Observations and Statements.

IROS's are a way for you to graphically document a new idea for captivation, attention-grabbing, deep-discussion, or connection and allows you to record the attempt made, the honest reflection from your perspective, the observations and cues from the audience, and any similarities or differences you found. There is also a spot in this visual organizer to record which attempt you are making on a particular idea.

For example, you might have had an amazing idea that you were convinced was going to work, but it fell flat. You realize the mistake you made, made the adjustments, and tried it again. This would version 2.0. You made a new iteration to an original idea and wanted to document progress. This visual organizer allows you to do so.

The concept behind IROS's is very similar to TMS's, but the organization scheme is a bit different. It is more horizontal in its approach and is filled out in a left-to-right fashion. I have provided an example below.

Table 5: Ideas, Reflections, and Observation Statements (IROS) Organizer

Version (Attempt)	Audience Component	Idea (I)	Reflection (R)	Observations (O)	Statements of Similarities or Differences (S)
1.0	Captivation -Engagement	To captivate my audience, I am going to remember everyone's names in the first five minutes by using association.	Out of the 20 students in my class, I forgot 4. I was disappointed because as soon as they said their names, I remembered.	Students were still impressed. They liked the idea that I took the time to try to get the names right and thought it was exciting.	I was more disappointed than they were. They seemed to like the brief activity, so I am going to proceed forward on the next day and make sure I get all 20 correct tomorrow.

Benefits of IROS

This template does a few things for you. First, it works as a tracker for you to remember what you have tried and what you are willing to try again. Having a track record of successes and failures shows where you have been and where you would like to go next in advancing your teaching practices. It shows your growth. The whole purpose of reading this book is to become a better educator. What better way to understand your growth than to display your ideas?

Second, using IROS on your ability to define the first two "C's" – *command* and *change*. You can fully identify whether the idea you tried to implement succeeded, failed, or landed somewhere in between. You can even go deeper to find out if the idea you implemented leads to becoming a strength that you can apply to your S-TMS's, a weakness that you can apply direct and immediate changes to your C-TMS's, or maybe you decide to scrap the idea altogether. Remember: Knowing what kind of educator you are can also occur by learning what kind of educator you are not.

Third, it provides a means to build on the third "C" – *Confidence*. Do you recall when we discussed the target for the "C of Selfs?" This functions as your self-assessment. You can assess your practices based on your perceptions and the perceptions of others. If you perform multiple iterations of this idea and make changes, it also serves as a self-discipline tracker. Practice enough, and you gain self-efficacy to utilize this idea anytime you want.

Fourth, it ensures you are keeping your own thoughts in check. Sometimes we think we are doing incredible work and our students are not seeing it through the same lens. Other times, we are beating ourselves up for something we tried, but our students come back and tell us how much they loved the idea and would like to see it more.

For as many educators I have met over the last decade and a half, I have found that we are our own toughest critics. IROS allows more objective clarity by observing what our students are noticing, while reserving our own perspectives before attempting to become the final judge, jury, and executioner.

Lastly, the IROS organizer provides an opportunity for you to promote further dialogue and pay it forward to other educators. Having others see your progress as a teacher empowers them to act. Teaching is a world of support and IROS fosters that support in growth of many, not just one. These can be opportunities to sit down with an organizational leader, mentor, coach, or another professional and discuss what your perceptions are. They might have some insights from their own observations that you can share with others.

Don't Forget: It's About Growth and Balance!

Much like The Voyage Inward, the overall goal is growth and balance. Progress, not perfection. The biggest difference between The Voyage Inward and The Voyage Outward is that your audience is not seeing the progress you are making. Instead, they will notice the results of the effort and the dedication you are showing toward their growth. After all, that is the exact reason we got into the field of Education: To help others grow.

The tricky part about The Voyage Outward is that you only find out whether you are making true growth by observing their learning outcomes and overall feedback. The students are not seeing your growth, even though they are such a powerful factor in shaping it.

This is where the next three "C's" come into play. You will know whether you are *captivating* their attention by their level of participation and engagement. You will know whether they are *clearly* grasping the material and the underlying messages in your lessons by their performance on future assessments and achievements. Most importantly, you will know whether you *connected* with them on a deeper level by the audience's testimonials, thank-you statements, and words or actions of appreciation down the road.

I will finish this chapter by sharing a story. When I was first hired as a teacher, my first year started in the middle, as I inherited an 8th grade

English/Language Arts group of students in North Carolina from a teacher who left for another position. I didn't have the opportunity to spend two weeks going through processes, policies, and procedures. I was convinced that I just needed to survive that year, then the next year will be more impactful.

I started by going through my expectations, goals, and objectives and focused strictly on their needs and what I could do to help them be successful in the year. Notice that I didn't emphasize content. It was valuable for them to learn; it was more valuable to find out their underlying needs. I spent a lot of time on The Voyage Inward as I was maneuvering through The Voyage Outward. It felt like I was flying by the seat of my pants. There were many things I was doing well and there were many timed I needed to make quick adjustments. Simply put, I was trying my absolute best to define who I was as a teacher and aligning those principles to their expectations. The long-term impact was too far out of view.

I asked them questions about what they thought of the activities, discussions, lessons, and other miscellaneous ideas. I documented all of them and wrote them down in my journal. I reflected on my own views and compared them to their observations. To be honest, this was the best decision I could have ever made.

I relocated to Pennsylvania years later, but before I did, I attended their high school graduation. You wouldn't believe the thank-you's, hugs, tears, gifts, and acts of kindness they showed me. To be honest, my first years of teaching English/Language Arts is an underlying reason why I decided to share my knowledge. I created an impact in a time that you would never expect a new teacher to do so.

To this day, they still reach out to me on social media, sharing the stories of impact that I had. What they didn't know is the impact they had on my growth and balance as an educator. They shaped me to be the educator I am today.

This is the exact reason why I am writing and sharing with you. You never know the impact you will have or the impact that others will have on you. However, the more that you document, ask questions, and track your practices as an educator, the more balance and growth you will find. More importantly, if you continue to focus on *engagement, depth, alignment,* and *trust* when you sail those three "C's" of *captivation, clarity, and connection,* you will find a deeper impact on your audience that will shape your practices for years to come. It will create a ripple effect in the water that will last a lifetime.

Hopefully, this story sheds some light on the power you can have if you truly examine your practices and openly communicate your vision with your audience. We will talk more about this in the upcoming chapters. Without further ado, let's take this positivity and roll into the waters of the fourth "C" – *Captivation!*

CHAPTER 7:
THE FOURTH "C" - CAPTIVATION

The first ten minutes of every lesson set the experience for the rest of the day. I will repeat: The first ten minutes of every lesson set the experience for the rest of the day.

Think about it: How many times have you sat in a class and you knew in the first ten minutes the experience you were going to get? How did it impact the rest of your day?

When you have passengers aboard your ship, you as the captain must not only tell them what to expect, but also show them what experiences they are going to have, and how you are going to deliver this to them. A captain is not only the leader, he or she is an entertainer of sorts too.

As a passenger, you know immediately whether you feel comfortable with the captain's ability to get you there safely while still making sure you have a good time. As a student or audience member, you know in the first ten minutes whether your learning experience is going to be captivating or dilapidating.

Much like the captain, you must possess the ability as an educator to know in advance the ways you are going to grab your audience's attention and captivate them.

On the surface, *captivation* is about the level of attention your audience is experiencing. As we explore this concept further, you will find that *captivation* feels so much more meaningful than that. It is about *invested attention.* True *captivation* occurs when the audience not only is giving you their eyes and ears, but they are giving you their feelings, observations, insights, beliefs, humor, personality, and values.

This feels a lot like *connection*, right? If this is so profound, why not just start there and skip *captivation* altogether?

Because before you create a meaningful impact with every individual on a deeper level (Sixth "C" – *Connection*), they need to deem you as a credible expert and believe the message is valuable (Fifth "C" – *Clarity*). Before they consider you as a credible expert and believe the message is valuable, they need to know immediately that their time will be well spent and will be worthwhile. This is the exact reason that I have labeled the Fourth "C" as *Captivation*. If you do not have the audience's eyes and ears, you will never fully have their brains or hearts and they will never get to a more significant level of trust with you.

Attention is such an underrated asset to have when you are building rapport with other people. If you have someone's attention, you gain the ability to change lives. *Captivation* gives you "the in" with other people. It provides you an initial contact point to show them you are invested in them and their learning.

More importantly, when you have someone's attention, they remember the impact you have had on them. There are still children I taught that mention a corny dad joke, a hug when they were feeling blue, or a powerful lesson that they still remember. There are still adults that took a dynamic tenet of leadership class that they still apply in their professional adventures. That would have never happened if those first ten minutes of the day were not prepared and executed appropriately. Age doesn't matter here; everyone wants an amazing experience, and you have ten minutes to deliver it to them or they are out.

How do you get their attention and keep it? How are you going to ensure that you not only engage your audience, but begin to form depth, alignment, and trust as well? This is where the four components of *Audience* shine.

Tying Captivation to CYA and the Four Components of Audience

Once again, we are going to prepare our ship. Instead of making sure that everything works, however, we are going to ensure that our passengers are comfortable, entertained, and happy during the voyage. We are going to view the best approaches associated with the four components of the CYA Model of Preparation, but this is about knowing your *audience* in how you exhibit *engagement, depth, alignment,* and *trust.* The purpose of *Command* and these four components allows you to understand and apply strategies to transmit meaningful energy to others in an educational setting.

As previously mentioned in Chapter 6, the four components of *Audience* are valuable because all four are applied in each "C," but they shift in importance as the chapters progress. For example, although you are working on *depth, alignment,* and *trust* with your audience, the most important factor here will be *engagement.* We will discuss how you can captivate your audience and build each of the other components while doing so. However, if you miss the *engagement* component during your lesson delivery, the other three components are highly unlikely to be achieved.

For example, let's say I try an *engagement* tactic where I do a brain teaser activity in the beginning of a critical thinking lesson, and it works. When the activity works, you will have a greater likelihood to go deeper with the lesson and find out more specified needs that they may need with critical thinking. You can use the activity as an anchor for the students to reflect and tie back to prior learning. If they are captivated with *engagement*, they are more likely to open up, ask additional questions, take an additional risk, and inquire about opportunities to learn something meaningful.

More so, you will also be able to subtly build alignment between your critical thinking lesson and their need to be better critical thinkers. You have more information you know is coming from your lesson that you can directly apply to their needs. This is a crucial opportunity for you to start forming the bridge with your audience and show them how the content you are teaching them will apply to their overall benefit in their daily lives. This provides an opportunity for more meaningful growth because it shows them that you are on the voyage with them. They are not alone.

Lastly, you can subconsciously begin to build trust with your audience because they know you are invested in their learning and engagement. They may not trust you to take care of their money or trust you with their darkest secrets, but they will trust you enough to confide in you their potential weakness that they recognize and need to change. This goes beyond rapport. They *trust* you with their internal processes and their insecurities. This is power.

This is exactly why *captivation* matters. In this "C," the audience is not going to fully trust you with everything they do, feel, or believe, but you can begin to scratch the surface by exciting them and essentially set up a building block to provide more meaning for them later.

For each of the four components of *Audience*, you are going to complete a row in Appendix C for IROS, documenting the occurrence with your observations. An example will be provided for each. Let's explore each of these components more in detail.

Captivation and Engagement

Captivation is critical when it comes to engagement. We have already discussed the importance of the first ten minutes of your day but determining how and what to prepare for your audience's engagement is going much elaborate. What specific techniques are you going to use to engage your audience?

First, let me stress that this is the reason the first three "C's" come first. If you do not know your strengths, then captivating your audience is out of the question. Ask yourself this question: *Where do I have Command with my four Yourself components that I can use to engage my audience?* This will be an amazing jump off point.

For example, if you are excellent with theatrics and you can use that in a direct lecture format, you might want to start with a one-person play for five minutes to captivate your audience. This will allow them to see that you are leaving yourself exposed and forces them to give something meaningful back to you.

On the other hand, if you are more inquisitive and like a break-out session for your groups, place them in small groups of four and start them on a scavenger hunt that will tie to your lesson a bit later. This will have them feel more control in their own well-being and show them in advance that investment is going to be an essential part of the course.

I am going to provide a more specific example where can you use a break-out group session to open an online synchronous class and do a scavenger hunt in an online setting. The purpose of this activity is to not only to familiarize themselves with the learning environment, but also to have them become more comfortable with their peers as they get to know the platform.

I have documented each of the steps in the IROS organizer (Table 6). I entered it as the first time I attempted this activity, with a focal point on *engagement*. Once you prepare and deliver, you are going to document your own personal reflections and their observations. I provided an example response. Lastly, I have displayed the similarities and differences between my personal reflections and the audience's observations:

Table 6: IROS Organizer for Captivation and Engagement

Version (Attempt)	Audience Component	Idea (I)	Reflection (R)	Observations (O)	Statements of Similarities or Differences (S)
1.0	Captivation -Engagement	To captivate my audience, I am going to start my lesson with a scavenger hunt to get to know the online platform. A treasure map will be shared to make it more interesting and fun.	Out of the 15 students in my class, everyone participated. There wasn't a reward, and I should have included an incentive. I think that they knew that I wanted them to feel comfortable with using the environment. I like that as a first attempt, I went with a strategy that didn't feel like too much of a stretch, but still pulled me out of my comfort zone.	The students enjoyed the map activity and the scavenger hunt. Used their cameras and were smiling and talking as a team. They especially liked that it was a team exploration. They would have liked an incentive. One group had difficulty with using technology and made jokes. I think they were embarrassed, but I showed them support and they felt more at ease.	Similarities are that an incentive was missing and needs to be included the next time I use this engagement strategy. Overall, students appreciated the effort, liked the length, and this will be a technique I use in the future. The group that struggled had a different experience with me because we bonded during the support that I provided for them. Overall, I believe that this first attempt was a success, but I just needs some minor tweaks with incentives and more investment in the discussions for those who are successful.

Notice in this example that there were many aspects of this opening engagement activity that went right. There were some minor adjustments to be made, but from observing the audience, getting feedback, and paying attention to our own reflections, this example could be used again in this scenario. That is what IROS does; it documents the process of transmission in the event and allows you to live in the moment as a component is occurring. It is the deepest sense of metacognition coming into fruition.

More importantly, it most likely went well because it was something you were comfortable with. You were confident and you had command over the topic. The audience is going to pay close attention to whether you know what you are doing and whether you are making a strong effort to connect with them. What is also important is you immediately recognize where *change* is needed.

If you know where you have *command*, you will know how to *captivate*. It is simply funneling that vision for what you are good at, immediately showcasing *confidence* in your ability to engage, showing off your talents, and building immediate engagement with your audience.

The question is this: Was your audience *captivated*? Pay attention to what happens immediately after you get feedback. Ask them what they thought of the activity. Tell them you were trying something different and you wanted to hear their perspectives. This will show the level of *engagement* you truly found in this approach. If you truly engaged, you would have a better likelihood to go *deeper* with their goals, needs, and insights in the future.

Captivation and Depth

The purpose behind *captivation* and *depth* is to provide further meaning. Although *captivation* ties more directly with *engagement*, you can still find opportunities throughout the experience to build on that initial activity With *depth*, the goal is to start with an activity and begin to go deeper with it in a more meaningful exercise.

If you did a breakout scavenger hunt in groups. in the first few minutes of class, you would want to build something into the scavenger hunt that would apply to a later lesson. Maybe as they are exploring the online component, they find a discussion question about the topic you are teaching. They may bring it up to you during class and you can excitingly tell them that you were saving that for later! Not only have you *captivated* their attention, but you have also given them something that they can look forward to later in the session.

Depth is about allowing them to find some meaning behind the activity and ask more insightful questions about the activity you just provided. It engages them to further their learning and want to explore as deeply as they can go. This enhances the *captivation* factor.

You may or may not have a separate IROS for this activity, but you can add some reflections or observations for *depth* opportunities in the organizer. For example, for *observations*, you might jot down that two students found a discussion question in the chat and were curious. You played up that curiosity with excitement and they became more *captivated* to discuss later.

The more you document, the better you will feel afterward. Everything becomes clearer in what you had true *command* over, what *changes* you have considered, and how *confident* you felt. More importantly, you will already see opportunities with the students in which you can make a deeper connection with earlier in the lesson. This allows for real connection to begin, which we will discuss further in Chapter 9.

Captivation and Alignment

The relationship between *captivation* and a*lignment* becomes a little bit trickier because you are aligning what they found to be meaningful with the activity with what you found to be meaningful. This is where you get to know your audience on a deeper level. This is tough to do in the first ten minutes with *captivation*, however, by asking them for direct and honest feedback, you can show them appreciation and show them that they are important to your growth, just as you are important to theirs.

As you can see, you can make a more meaningful relationship when both parties have a stake in the process. If you are simply talking at them, they don't feel *engaged*, they won't seek *depth*, and they won't want to *align* with you. That is why paying close attention to the "S" in IROS is important. It allows for you to see where your principles and their principles align in a specific space.

For example, in the Statements section, it was discussed that students and I both felt that incentives were necessary. This is a perfect opportunity to showcase that alignment between your thoughts and theirs. It also gives you the opportunity to thank them for their feedback and to mention that you genuinely appreciate it. This shows them that you both are *aligned* in their desire to learn and participate.

You may make an additional note in the "S" section that when you thanked the students, one student said some kind words back and loved that you cared about being better as a teacher. This *captivates* the audience, not because of the activity, but by your desire to have them involved in success. Write those notes down too! These notes are valuable pieces of information that you can use in the future and it can reassure you that you are doing something positive in your daily teaching practices.

Notice with *captivation*, the process becomes very clear with the visual from the last chapter: The deeper we go, the less it is about the activity and the more it becomes about the dynamic relationship between you and the audience. It is more personalized. This is critical toward your success on The Voyage Outward. Now that we have discussed the first three *Audience* components with *captivation*, let's discuss the toughest one: *Trust*.

Captivation and Trust

The relationship with *captivation* and *trust* is small, but that doesn't mean it cannot be established with the audience. Trust is built through multiple actions that are genuine in nature. If you build an activity where you can allow flexibility, allow them to make mistakes, and allow them to believe that you are supporting them, the chances are extremely high that you are building an underlying trust with them. We will discuss how you can make more meaningful strides of trust in Chapter 9.

For example, maybe a group in your online class mentions that they are struggling to find three different areas in the scavenger hunt. They tell you that they "are not strong with technology" and that they are "computer illiterate." They make jokes about themselves on the surface, but under the surface, you can see that there is slight embarrassment.

Listen closely and observe these behaviors. This is a key opportunity to show them that you are supporting them. Ask them guiding questions to help them get there. Once they get all aspects of the scavenger hunt, do a happy dance, and show them that you are proud that they worked through adversity. Most importantly, tell them that you got through it together! The more that you show that *alignment* in a situation, the more likely they are going to trust you over the course of the experience.

Once again, jot these things down in the IROS table! They are critical observations that you can use later for future lessons.

Although you are focusing on *engagement* with them, on a more meaningful level they *trust* that you are going to support them if they are struggling with anything. They are *captivated* by your willingness to positively encourage them to succeed. This is a huge step, even if minimal, because it provides further opportunity to build more trust with them over a lesson. The most important thing is to find as many opportunities to build trust as you can because they are rare to find when you are focusing on *captivation*. If you find an opportunity, seize it immediately!

Captivation and Social Cues

As you can see, *captivation* has the most immediate impact on *engagement*, but the other three components can be indirectly affected by *captivation* as well. If you are looking closer, you can see that paying attention to social cues allows you to truly see *how* you are engaging your audience. How immersed is your audience?

To find this out, you are going to need to pay attention to the social cues your audience is providing. This is why the "O" in IROS is so important; you must *observe* the clues that the audience is transmitting back to you. Transmission is a two-way street. It is easy to only focus on how you are transmitting energy; it is much more difficult to see how your audience is receiving you and how they are transmitting the energy back to you. The observations of the verbal and non-verbal cues will give you that information.

Think about this: If they are dialed into your activity, then they are *captivated* through impactful *engagement*. If they are dialed into the underlying message of the activity and what meaning they can get out of it, then they are *captivated* by the overall *depth*. If they are dialed in to how you are meeting their needs through the activity and subsequent discussions, then they are *captivated* by the *alignment* provided. Lastly, if they are dialed into you as a person, and believe you are going to genuinely and holistically focus on their best interest, then they are not only *captivated* by you, they *trust* you.

When viewing how *captivated* your audience is, observe their body posture, their inflection in their voices, their excitement in the chat, their facial expressions, their eyes, their lips, their hands, their pitch. If you observe that an audience member is going to their cell phone, looking off camera, talking to someone else, staring at the ceiling, rubbing their eyes, yawning, speaking in a monotone delivery, or just emotionally distant, then make a shift. Make an adjustment. Do something because they are not captivated.

As mentioned earlier, *captivation* is about *invested attention*. There is belief behind the cues. There is a desire that they want to go on the voyage with you. Your Voyage Outward is causing them to want to go on their own Voyage Inward. You already know how important the Reflection portion of IROS is; you focused heavily on those pieces in your Voyage Inward. The Observation portion shows how your attempts impact the students' behaviors and perceptions of the task. Take full advantage of your observations because it will be an essential guide that shows you the next direction to move. It is your map to the next destination of creating a more meaningful impact.

Now that you can take the important steps to *captivate* your audience on multiple levels, the path toward *connection* is much more straightforward. Your Voyage Outward is ready for the next "C." It is time to achieve *clarity* with your audience.

CHAPTER 8:
THE FIFTH "C" - CLARITY

Now that we have created a foundation for the way we are building trust with our audience, it is time to go deeper. It is time to ensure that there is *clarity* in the message you are providing.

To be clear, I do not mean *clarity* in the content, as if to say that the lesson must make sense. I mean *clarity* as in the message is clear in how the information and presentation of the material is going to benefit them personally. It must ignite a more profound spark for them to seek further exploration of their current thinking and processing. It must be worthwhile. Think of it this way: If *captivation* from the last chapter was about invested attention, then *clarity* is about invested *value*.

As it was previously mentioned, The Voyage Outward is about the eye of the beholder. *Value* is going to look differently to everyone. The only way you can determine value for each individual is to go for *depth*. You must ask more meaningful questions, open more meaningful dialogue, seek deeper relationships, and exert energy to look under the surface. You explore their *WIIFM* – "What's In It for Me?" and match it. You are showing your audience you *value* who they are as people, while also showing them that they should *value* what you have to offer.

One question I have contemplated myself during this process is this: "What if my audience values logic and knowledge more than anything else?" Yes, your content knowledge matters, but how you showcase that knowledge in a way that is applicable and relevant becomes more important. No matter which way you investigate, *depth* is critical for success.

You must determine what it is that lights your students' fires. Do they get excited when you share a meaningful story? Do they question facts or bring in new facts as you are discussing? Do they love a good quote? Do they love to be heard when meaningful reflections come about? These are the observations you need to find as you get to know the students and what they hope to achieve.

As I mentioned in the fourth "C" – *captivation*, sometimes you must ask. You must address what their goals, needs, expectations, and purpose are to gain better insight about them. As important as it is to know your own strengths and areas of growth, it is equally as important to have students reflect on their strengths and areas of growth as well. This is what *depth* is all about: Getting below the surface.

But Wait! There's More...

That's right! *Clarity* not only focuses on the importance of establishing *depth* with your audience. It is a 2-for-1 special!

Clarity is a two-step process that not only causes you to identify your audience's goals, needs, expectations, and purpose; it helps you identify how you are going to take that information and show them how you are going to help them. This thought process requires you to think more critically because you are understanding the concept of *alignment*.

Alignment is the bridge that allows you to clearly show your audience that *you* are invested in their *value*. See what I did there?

Clarity of value is a two-way street. The audience must find value in the *depth* you are providing them AND they must see that you are creating *alignment* to their values through your ability to lead them. Together, these two components show your audience that you want to genuinely help them succeed. This is why *clarity* is so important; you are disclosing to every student that you clearly understand their individual needs and demonstrating to them that you are clearly going to show the way to achieve success.

Alignment creates a more streamlined approach to show the audience your level of respect. For decades, teachers have been told that they must always have complete control of their classroom environment. While this is true, what is not discussed is that *alignment* demonstrates that you can have complete control of the classroom without demanding it. You are taking the time to show the audience that all voices matter in the classroom dynamic. If there is a value that is important to them, you will go out of your way to make sure that their needs are met on their terms.

Unlike *captivation*, the proverbial "wow-factor" for *clarity* is not noticed on the surface. If you are *captivating*, the audience will immediately let you know if they are impressed by your *engagement* with them. They will see an initial investment.

Clarity is more deep-rooted in their ability to process the "wow-factor." They don't find the value in just the activities or initial investment anymore; that will fade. With *clarity*, they find a more meaningful value in you. This happens because they are *clear* in their understanding that you are reaching *deeper* to understand their needs and *aligning* your mission to meet and exceed those needs. This "wow-factor" occurs not because they are wow-ed by your preparation of material or building of activities, but because of your ability to meet them on a more introspective level they did not originally expect.

An example of establishing *clarity* is when you are monitoring a small group breakout session where they are discussing something of value. You ask the students a meaningful question about their thoughts on a heated topic. This could include topics of race, leadership, heroism, mental health, development, or many more. You have an idea that you are going to include a meaningful discussion where they can discuss any opinion freely without judgment. Much like Chapter 7 (and will be for Chapter 9), you are going to complete a row in Appendix C in the IROS graphic organizer, documenting the occurrence with your observations. An example will be provided for each. Let's explore each of these components more in detail.

Clarity and Engagement

Although *captivation* builds the closest relationship to *engagement*, *clarity* is still a necessity. With a more personal or touchy subject, you must set the boundaries in advance so that expectations are clear, the room for an open forum is established, and the room for comfort becomes more readily accessible.

When we use a potentially heated topic in a small group discussion with pointed questions, students have already practiced the breakout session once, so they have some familiarity. The concept here is to take something you know is of meaning to them and go deeper. I have taught many leadership topics where concepts like *diversity*, *culture*, and *generational* differences have become a focal point. You must be able to facilitate and navigate these discussions with clearly positive intent. You must also be able to clearly demonstrate that our original opinions are from experience, and if we do not share, we do not grow.

This type of *engagement* is very important to establish because when you dive into the open waters, you must make sure you anchor yourself to something meaningful. Setting the standards engages them to believe that they can safely share their unique perspectives without being demolished by others. The *clarity* for *engagement* lies in the expectations that you have previously built for the audience. If you did not establish this earlier, the mountain is much harder to climb.

Clarity and Depth

We have already discussed some key elements about the relationship between *clarity* and *depth*. Remember that the only way you can make the most meaning to an individual is to go for *depth*. As previously mentioned, you are showing your audience you *value* who they are as people, while also showing them that they should *value* what you have to offer.

In this specific example for *depth*, you are asking intriguing questions on a concept of diversity for which you are trying to find more meaningful perspectives. You notice that your students might be a bit apprehensive at first, so you open yourself up a little to show them it is okay to test the waters. You also ask your audience to share a meaningful experience where they have either witnessed or been a part of something where diversity that was either positively or negatively used. This is *depth* because you are no longer focusing on a general topic, but their intrinsic perspectives on that topic.

By making a valiant attempt at this discussion in a small group environment, you can monitor the way the discussion is opening up and facilitate where needed. If the group is already comfortable with sharing, *depth* becomes more natural. Share your positive feedback with them, thank them for their contributions in an authentic manner and consider asking an additional guiding question to move the conversation forward.

However, if you have a group that might not be as comfortable, they might ask what you are looking for. You might have to rephrase your question, share a story about yourself, open up more meaningful dialogue, or provide a relevant personal example. In any case, your goal is to provide *clarity* and model what *depth* looks like. If you are sharing, more of them will share as well. This is where you can go deeper and show them that you *clearly* value their insights.

For *clarity* and *depth*, I have documented each of the steps in the IROS organizer below (Table 7). Although we have done breakouts before, this is the first breakout attempt that I am attempting with an emphasis on *depth*. In addition, because *depth* and *alignment* are essential to *clarity*, I am going to label and document insights on both.

Once you prepare and deliver, you are going to document your own personal reflections and their observations. I provided an example response.

Lastly, I have displayed the similarities and difference between my personal reflections and the audience's observations:

Table 7: IROS Organizer for Clarity, Depth and Alignment

Version (Attempt)	Audience Component	Idea (I)	Reflection (R)	Observations (O)	Statements of Similarities or Differences (S)
1.0	Clarity – Depth and Alignment	To show clarity with my audience, I am going to discuss a more heated topic with diversity, and clearly show and model how to share experiences in a small group setting. This should not only provide depth in the sharing of insights, but I can show them alignment in my ability to show them that I have experiences worth sharing as well. This will show that we all face issues with this topic.	Out of the 15 students in my class, everyone participated. I broke them into groups of 3 because it would allow for more time for each person to speak. Then I brought everyone back and had each group share their findings with a whiteboard displayed. I believe this went really well because 9-10 students opened up immediately, and when one group had a tough time in the beginning, I shared my insights and they felt much more comfortable.	Students thoroughly enjoyed this activity and said it was nice because they face this issue a lot in their experiences. They had differing perspectives, but they said they didn't feel judged. One debate got a little heated and required a little more facilitation, but I was positive and genuinely appreciated their passion. They understood that we are all in this together and one student said they wish they had more opportunities in their daily lives to do this exercise. Many more students agreed with that sentiment.	Similarities are very close in this case because I wanted to set a clear expectation, put them in small groups, and allow them to have the floor. The only difference is that I learned some groups require a little bit more probing when it comes to depth, and others need you to share first to create more meaningful alignment. I will absolutely use this strategy in the future, and I think that for tomorrow's class, I will review this discussion with them as a reminder of the positivity we gained by doing so. Hopefully, this will help them to trust me and each other even more.

Notice in this example that there were many aspects of this deeper activity that went really well. In the observations, some groups naturally achieved greater *clarity* in the underlying meaning and created alignment with each other. Other groups needed the facilitator to model *clarity* to them and build alignment amongst everyone.

I know what you are thinking: What happens if it doesn't work out like this? Believe me, sometimes that happens. Let's say in this example that you thought the lesson went well, but one group shared only on the surface and said they wish they would have had more time or more examples. Another group felt uncomfortable sharing because one member didn't believe that diversity was important, and you weren't there to hear it.

These things happen, but the idea is to recognize, discuss, adapt, and retry. If this situation would have happened, I would have documented those differences in the "S" column, and I would have revised my questioning strategies and invented new ideas to help facilitate the discussion more. I would pay attention to more characteristics during introductions and I would maybe readjust the way I am building groups because of it. Maybe I create pairs instead of groups of three. The fact that you are making *changes* means you are growing. Therefore The Voyage Inward must come first.

Most importantly, I would have created another IROS with a second attempt in the future to see what progress was made. I mentioned this earlier, and it still holds true: *It's about progress, not perfection.* Progress creates *clarity* because it shows you where you have been and where you need to move forward. Let's discuss the second part of this IROS example with *alignment*.

Clarity and Alignment

In this IROS example, you not only built in an opportunity for others to discuss a more meaningful topic in *depth*, but you also allowed for *alignment* to occur as well. First, you created a sense of alignment by having each group share their insights to find alignment amongst themselves. They began to believe that they are not alone in their deeper, more intrinsic thoughts.

Furthermore, because you had the opportunity to share a relevant story or experience, you were able to demonstrate to them that you were *aligned*, not in the topic, but in the notion that you all might have been a bit uncomfortable and still decided to share.

It is crucial that, as a facilitator, you must be able to *align* their perspectives to others' perspectives and your own in the discussion. For example, I am an older millennial who is White, American, and a bit more privileged than others. I must understand that my perspectives are not going to be the same as others, but I need to listen to them for more meaning and align my principles with theirs. My recognition of my own limitations, while still showing my audience that I am growing as a human being allows for *alignment* to occur. Yes, I may be an expert on the topic and a facilitator, but I make a strong attempt to *align* my humanistic qualities to theirs and show them that we are all people.

As I mentioned in the previous chapter, more meaningful relationships are built when both parties have stake in the process of sharing. For example, in the Statements section, it was discussed that students and I both shared that it was nice to have the opportunity to openly discuss a tough topic when it is such a hot issue and there typically is not a space to reflect and share.

The reason *clarity* becomes so valuable here is because it is *clear* to them that you understand they had a need to openly share their insights and that you were aligned with them in the sharing process. You have *clearly* defined that this classroom dynamic is one that is a safe space to openly share viewpoints without judgment and that power can come from those discussions. This is why *clarity* is so profound; when you create this space through *alignment*, you have the opportunity to build more meaningful *connections* and truly create a sense of *trust*.

Clarity and Trust

As previously discussed, *trust* is built through actions that are authentically shown to your audience. Doing a breakout discussion of this magnitude will not immediately establish *trust*, but it will absolutely carry you further toward it. Having one successful discussion like this will not create trust with everyone, but maybe for a few, it will create a more transparent space to allow them to be themselves.

However, if you built in opportunities to establish greater *depth* and *alignment*, the likelihood of you building *trust* more quickly becomes an inevitability. If *trust* is created through actions, and you are clearly demonstrating to them, time and time again, that you are creating an open, honest space to discuss their insights, experiences, and stories, your path to *trust* is a more direct and straight one.

The trick with this is to seek ideas for *clarity* to occur. It is going to take multiple activities that showcase *depth* and *alignment* to their values to display that you are trustworthy to them. The further down the triangle of *Audience* you want to go, the more dedication and preparation needs to be considered.

A Final Note on Clarity

Just in case you are not seeing a pattern yet, I am going to provide a final dose of *clarity* for you. The deeper and more individualized you are in seeking meaningful, mutually beneficial relationships with your audience, the greater impact you are going to have on your audience and what they can achieve in their future endeavors.

This type of commitment takes an incredible level of energy, practice, and dedication to achieve. This is typically the exact reason why some educators are fine with being decent and going no further. They are content with teaching the class in a whole group setting, staying within the lines of discussion, and staying within their comfort zones with creating new activities.

But that's not you. If it were, you would have set this book down a long time ago.

The question is this: How far are you willing to go to create a more significant impact? If you are genuinely excited about this, you are ready for the sixth "C" – *Connection*. You will learn my deepest secrets that have allowed me to connect with thousands of students over the last decade and a half. This upcoming chapter is where I provide my most memorable stories, experiences, insights, reflections, tears, excitement, and passion. It is truly the reason why I get up every day.

If this excites you, then you have absolutely enjoyed reading so far and I ask you to keep reading. If you are up to the challenge, get ready for the vastest of waters! Onto the "C" of *connection* we go!

CHAPTER 9:
THE SIXTH "C" - CONNECTION

Brace yourself: This "C" is a heavy one. In my honest appraisal of education in the 21st Century, *Connection* - the sixth "C" - is the difference between those who leave a lasting impression on their students and those who don't. This "C" is the reason that educators win awards, get recognized as accomplished or distinguished educators, help other teachers succeed, and most importantly, make a difference in the lives of others.

Connection is the reason that I still speak to my middle school and high school students to this day. They reach out and want me to be proud of them, even though they are nearly thirty years old. It is also the reason that Fortune 500 and Fortune 1000 companies still reach out to me to deliver powerful leadership trainings, guide them toward better courses, and ultimately *trust* that I can help them create powerful business relationships. Whether you are eight or eighty years old, you want to be able to *connect* with another person.

Connection is critical to everyone's success. It builds opportunity for long-term *trust* to occur and creates life-long memories shared between you and another person. They remember you not who you were a teacher, but who you were as a human being and how you helped them become better human beings. Because of this, *connection* is the most important "C" that you can learn in your voyages.

Wait, wait, wait. If this is the most important "C," why is it not listed as the first "C?" Because you cannot achieve *connection* without being able to have *command* of your strengths, *change* in your behavior and growth, *confidence* in your abilities and practice, *captivation* of your audience to establish your "in" with them, and *clarity* in the messaging and coalition you are building with them. *connection* only happens when those first five "C's" have been subconsciously noticed by your audience. It is a deeper kind of education that requires time, energy, and sincerity.

More importantly, you cannot know how to build *trust* with other people if you do not *trust* yourself in your teaching practices. You also cannot build *trust* with other people if you do not know how to *engage, build depth,* and *align* your principles with theirs. This is essential to building a more meaningful *connection*, but you must learn to crawl and then to walk, before learning how to run effectively.

When we discussed the visual in Chapter 6 where we maneuver from *engagement* to *trust*, the visual becomes narrower as it progresses deeper. In Figure 4 (next page), I have provided more explanation about how the fourth, fifth, and sixth "C" function closely with the four components of *Audience*.

Engagement is meant to hit the masses; it is meant to be broad and to build a surfaced bridge with the whole group. *Depth* and *alignment* start to uncover more specific needs, goals, fears, and attitudes about tough topics. *Trust* is individualized, distinct, and special in the way you *connect* with a single audience member. This means that you must get to know what makes each individual tick.

Figure 4: Four Components of Audience Triangle: Reviewed with "C's" 4-6
Amount of People Impacted

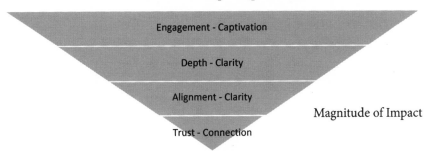

Magnitude of Impact

I should clarify from the visual that although you can achieve *engagement,* *depth, alignment,* and *trust* through *captivation, clarity,* and *connection,* I have previously mentioned that you have better opportunity and more chances to build *engagement* through *captivation* and *depth* and *alignment* through *clarity.*

This means that you are going to find the sixth "C" – *connection* is deeply joined with the underlying component of *trust.* If you can create meaningful *connections* during your lessons, each student will slowly begin to believe that you are wholeheartedly there to help them. *Trust* can take time to build, but if you seek opportunities to *connect* with another person on their terms, you have a much greater likelihood of earning their *trust.*

What is even more crucial to recognize here is that *connection* and *trust* are built on an individual basis. What *trust* looks like to one person may look completely different to another. If you have 20-30 students in your class, this will be mentally and emotionally exhausting. However, it will make an impact that resonates with your audience for a lifetime.

If this seems impossible, it is because concepts like *connection* and *trust* feel like intangible concepts that are more abstract than concrete. Luckily, you have come this far, so I am going to share a big secret with you that will allow you to find opportunities to build *trust* and make more lasting *connections* with each person in your class. It's time to turn on the GAS.

Connection and Trust: Brought to You by GAS

I told you I would share a couple of my deepest secrets in this book. The first is GAS. Genuine. Actionable. Steps.

GAS is about demonstrating an act toward another person to show them you are genuinely invested in their success. You cannot fake GAS. It is an entire shift in your mindset to be other-centered in every interaction.

To build on previous chapters: If *captivation* is about invested attention, and *clarity* is about invested value, then *connection* is about invested *loyalty*. You are taking a leap of faith to showcase to each member of your audience that your acts show *loyalty* to their needs, goals, and hopes in growing.

There are several ways you can show your audience that you can be trusted, but you need to find out what makes them value trust. You could provide extra time to talk to a student, listen sincerely when they open up to you, provide help when they are unsure, making concepts more relevant to them personally, learn about their culture, ask meaningful questions that are important to them, or show them through your passion that life is simply better when you are on the positive side of it.

For example, some students are very heavily focused on the accuracy of the content being provided. Because of this, they trust that you are a knowledge source of information. Other times, they see your passion for the delivery of the content, and they gravitate toward you. Because of this, they trust your dedication to the craft. Then there are those who value their interactions with you. They want to make sure that you care about them as a person, and not just a student. When you show them this emotional investment, they trust your ability to build relationships.

The trick to GAS is to first identify what makes the most meaning for each individual in your classroom, and then find actionable ways to demonstrate that you are invested. For me personally, I trust transparency more than anything. If you are interacting with me and you are hiding, omitting, or lying, I lose complete investment and you will not earn my trust. The most significant GAS that someone could apply here are:

1. Providing an open space to communicate openly with me

2. Demonstrating respect during discussion

3. Telling me upfront if there is information they do not know

4. Finding out the information to make better meaning

These are intentional, actionable items that if shown genuinely, can be extremely powerful methods of building meaningful individual connection. If you are looking to build more significant, deeper trust, then you shouldn't seek to do this once or twice, but every time. After all, *connection* is about going deeper. GAS allows you to demonstrate in every instance that you deserve their *trust*.

Additional GAS's include buying students a small gift, helping them through a tough personal issue, having them open up in a meaningful discussion, telling them you truly believe in them, helping them discover their own personal strength, being positive and honest, being transparent and vulnerable, showing you are an expert in knowledge and willing to share, and so much more. Basically, if you are genuine and you seize opportunities to do something impactful for another individual, the likelihood of gaining their trust becomes much easier.

To provide a meaningful example, I observed an online, synchronous course being taught by a fellow colleague, and her student was having a ton of difficulty with their internet connection. They lost approximately thirty minutes of valuable instruction by helping him troubleshoot. The instructor saw that the student was visibly upset on camera and was worried about what was missed. First, the student apologized several times, but the instructor calmly said, "No problem at all. We will get through this together." To me, that was inspiring.

What impressed me most was that the instructor not only helped the student through the issue, she also recapped some information to bring the student up to speed. She allowed an opportunity and the student to meet with her for fifteen minutes after the class was finished. The student immediately grinned, felt a lot better, and the issue was resolved. She took a chance to calmly help the student through the vulnerability, stay positive in the moment, and provide additional care after the fact.

While this may look like *clarity*, the instructor showed a deeper level of *connection* because she took a genuine approach not only to get her student the missed information, but also used GAS effectively to demonstrate actions worth purpose. First, she took the time to show her student that she cares about his success. Second, she took action to ensure the student knew she went out of her way. Lastly, she took greater opportunity to build more meaning in their dynamic relationship in those fifteen minutes after class. This is where power lives. A framework of *trust* was immediately built and grown, and it only took fifteen minutes.

The reason that GAS is so powerful is this: If you take genuine, actionable steps to impact another person, they will believe you will do it again. They have faith in you, not only as their educator, but as a human being. Just make sure that if something like this were to happen again, that you follow up and follow through. This level of commitment to GAS shows that no matter what, you are invested.

Even though it may not seem like it, *trust* is being built during *engagement*, *depth*, and *alignment* because it follows the premise of vulnerability. When something awful occurs, you have the ability in those moments to build *connection* before it gets to *trust*. This is because you are basically walking them through three types of *connection*:

1. I am going to connect with you on identifying the problem. (*Engagement*)

2. I am going to connect with you on how I can get you through the problem. (*Depth*)

3. I am going to connect with you and show you that I have been there before and that you are not alone. (*Alignment*)

Now that we provided a critical example, let's break down how each component of *Audience* coordinates with GAS and the "C" of *connection*. In this case, the student feels extremely embarrassed and rather than sitting in discomfort, you should seize the opportunity to use it to build trust.

Connection and Engagement

As previously mentioned, *captivation* holds the closest relationship to *engagement*, but it is *connection* that shows a more profound sense of *engagement*. It is not about the *engagement* into the content; it is strictly about being in open waters together while the sharks are circling. This is truly *focused* and *emotional engagement* occurring.

In this case, the instructor provided a sense of comfort in a time of vulnerability. Even though the ship began to sink momentarily, she played the role of the captain and said, "I have been here before and we will get through this." She put herself in the student's shoes, felt the embarrassment too, and still managed to *connect* with the student and make a more meaningful impact. At the very least, the student would be currently *engaged* into the problem with the instructor.

This type of *engagement* is very important to establish because there is no more room to miss. The instructor also found opportunities to still *engage* the student with the content by recapping the information. The student has officially gone overboard and is swimming without a raft or life jacket in the open water. The student is at the instructor's mercy to help get him through this in a meaningful way, so at this point, the student needed to be invested. She showed the student that she was going to help him get through it, one way or another, and the student believed it. The instructor was far from settled with handling a rough morning but at this point, an emotional level of *engagement* has been established because the student has nowhere else to go besides working with the instructor to get through it.

Connection and Depth

Connection and *depth* also have a relatively meaningful impact because it is on you to establish a sense of priority to resolve a concern. If *engagement* says, "I recognize that this is a concern for you," then *depth* says, "I *truly want* to help you get out of this and *we* are going to do it together." Finding a *deeper connection* is also emotional because it is not just about getting the problem fixed, but intentionally showing the student GAS by focusing on the individual relationship between instructor and student.

An underlying sense of *depth* was built in this example because the student mentioned that their internet connection was not working, which helped the instructor to begin troubleshooting and working through the issue at hand. The reason this is so valuable is because the teacher individualized the level of focus and made it a priority to find a resolution for the student, so that he can be involved in the class.

Furthermore, *depth* was created because the teacher went the extra mile to show the student that not only were we going to get the issue fixed, but that we were going to ensure that the student would not miss a thing. This level of *depth* is priceless because not only is the instructor throwing a life raft for a situation out of her control, but she is also making a valiant effort herself to pull him back to the ship.

This type of *depth* has nothing to do with vulnerability in the sense of speaking up. This is about saving a student from true loss and the fear of being lost. Because the instructor took that valuable moment to assure the student that everything was going to be handled well from start-to-finish, it allowed the student to feel safer with his vulnerability. This type of interaction is crucial because it notifies all parties that we need to get through fears to come out on the other side.

To be completely honest, using GAS intentionally in these moments not only shows one student that they can begin to trust you, but everyone else in the room begins to see it from an outsider's perspective. If they are paying attention, they may imagine themselves in the same situation and say,

"That is so good to know because I could lose internet connection too, and if that happened, I would be safe with this instructor." That kind of thinking not only allows you to *connect more deeply* with one audience member but allows you to *connect* on a surface level with the others as well.

Connection and Alignment

You just spent time building a *connection* through helping a student through a mentally and emotionally challenging process and you are now their hero! This is the time where you showcase that heroism further, right? No.

This is where you show humility and grace. This is where you show you students that this could happen to anyone of us. This is where you show *alignment*.

Connection and *alignment* almost sound synonymous with each other because they both achieve a sense of togetherness. They require you to show them that even though you are the captain on the ship, you are equally as vulnerable. You are *one voice of many*.

In this example, the instructor used her wisdom and calmness to *connect* with the individual on a deeper level and walk him through the issue. The *alignment* piece not only showed that the instructor "got the problem" but also showed that she "got the student." She demonstrated that they were not only *aligned* in the problem, but they were *aligned* in how easy this issue could happen to anyone and that no matter what, *we* will get through this.

Here is where *trust* begins to be built with a more significant purpose. The trick is that you must see what they see and value what they value. It evolves from the belief that the student will be helped to the belief that the student will be protected and not embarrassed. The one time the instructor had the opportunity to gloat, show power, and demonstrate true authority, and she instead showed modesty and benevolence. This aligned the student with the belief that although she threw the life raft, she did it because *she is one of us*.

Once again, notice the pattern here: The instructor *engaged* the problem with the student head-on, went into more meaningful *depth* to show him he was going to be taken care of, and then *aligned* herself to him in the premise that they were together in this issue. *Alignment* is strictly about finding common purpose between *us*.

Connection and Trust

The blessing and curse behind *connection* and *trust* is that you must get to know what makes the audience member *trust* in the first place, and then you need to decide how you build on that *trust*. *Trust* is about taking the leap of faith to be vulnerable and open about who you really are and hope that it is enough to *connect* with them.

Some people trust knowledge before anything else. This means that if they see you are an expert in your field, they are more likely to trust you. You would build GAS by providing research, data, facts, charts, and graphs. Others seek passion and enthusiasm behind the knowledge. If they see that you are genuinely passionate in your daily endeavors, spontaneous in your actions, and go the extra mile for them, they are more likely to trust you.

Most importantly, *trust* is about knowing you have something of meaning to offer them, and you willingly do so to build a stronger connection to them. *Trust* is built through selflessness. It is the reason that the most important teacher in your life still stands out today. They were most likely the ones who always did the right thing, spent the extra time, made the most meaning for you, and showed you something that you never saw in yourself. They knew *your* value and showed it to you through GAS.

The greatest purpose in how *connection* is established is that it stays singularly focused on one individual at a time, but still indirectly impacts the masses. If you try to *Connect* on a deeper level with every member at once, that *connection* becomes weaker. By taking an individualized approach to *connection*, the *trust* between those two people become extremely powerful, and the other students in the classroom will want that same *connection* to occur with them in the future.

To use the previous example, that instructor knew her student lacked confidence with technology, but had the potential to grow from it. She saw the opportunity and took a chance to *Connect*. She showed the student that, no matter what, *"I am here for you."* This is something the student valued, and the instructor seized upon it. She not only offered the extra time and assistance to make him feel comfortable, but also followed through on her promise. Her actions from start to finish were authentic and purposeful. They were selfless. These steps specifically demonstrated how GAS lit that student's fire.

GAS was shown multiple times in this interaction: The demonstration that they will get through fixing the internet issue, the recognition of why it frustrated the student, the alignment to show that it happens to everyone, the fact that she will not leave him behind, and the fact that she will provide the additional support to see it through with the student after class. The more GAS you provide in the interaction, the more that students are willing to open themselves up to you.

It is critical that when you see and make a strong attempt to build a deeper *connection* and establish *trust*, you document it. You must document so that you know how to reference it again if they feel that trust is lacking between you two. This is where IROS comes in. You list the GAS you provided in the Idea section, state why you chose that path in the Reflection section, list your Observations of their reactions, and show similarities of where *trust* has been built and possible next steps.

The interactions in the previous example are listed in the IROS Organizer for Connection and Trust, located in Table 8 on the next page:

Table 8: IROS Organizer for Connection and Trust

Version (Attempt)	Audience Component	Idea (I)	Reflection (R)	Observations (O)	Statements of Similarities or Differences (S)
1.0	Connection – Trust	One student has been struggling with online learning and the wireless connection. I noticed that if other applications are closed, his computer works faster. I can help him. Not only that, but I believe that I can build better trust with him by showing him that we are all going through this together and we will get through this together. I will help him get caught up by any means necessary.	I noticed that when I first helped him, he was ready to throw in the towel. He was visibly upset and felt hopeless. I noticed that when I was calm and positive, I was able to connect more with him. I felt more empowered because I was able to help him find strength.	When I offered to help him, he felt safer. When I followed through with helping him get caught up, I noticed that he was extremely thankful. He mentioned that he didn't want to be behind everyone else because of Wi-Fi. It seems that we were able to talk on a much deeper level about how he was feeling, and I noticed that my follow through made him more comfortable to talk to me.	There are now a lot of similarities between how I was feeling and how he was feeling. We both felt frustrated because of the modality not working. We both stayed calm and positive throughout and the deeper connection happened because he trusted me to get him through any issues, no matter what. The level of dedication is what he trusted and now I know how I can continue to build trust with him. I am going to check in with him tomorrow to see if he has any extra questions. This will continue show him the additional GAS!

These are the types of actions that make you a great educator. Not good, but great. When another person *trusts* you, you have built a *connection* that is extremely hard to break. They see you as a mentor, a leader, a human being, and a confidant, all in one form. Because of this, you have built something so deep that the student becomes your crusader. They want to become a champion for themselves and for you. They will follow you anywhere.

What Happens when Disconnect Happens: Find a CURE!

Obviously, the goal is to make sure that you have a strong *connection* and a significant level of *trust* with every member of your audience. But what happens when disconnect occurs?

Does your brain go here? *The ship is hit and is taking on a lot of water! There is no way that this can be fixed! Abandon ship, right?* Wrong.

Sometimes, even the best plans do not work the way you hope they would. No matter how well you prepare your ship, there will always be repairs and maintenance that must occur. Remember that repair on a ship and repair on *connection* have the same exact philosophy: *The earlier the intervention, the simpler the repair.*

What happens when the mistake is too massive to repair? It isn't. *The earlier the intervention, the simpler the repair.* What happens if I completely messed up? You didn't. *The earlier the intervention, the simpler the repair.*

Yes, you can also say "The more significant the damage, the more significant the repair." This is undeniable. However, the sooner you get working on the repair, the sooner the ship is essentially fixed.

In modern education, the dynamic of the teacher-student relationship is solely built on *trust*, and when that is damaged, it requires you to think and act fast on repairs. That is why I am sharing another of my deep secrets: An early intervention strategy to get back to *connection*. I call it the CURE. CURE stands for *Create, Uncover, Reconsider,* and *Express.*

Yes. It is another acronym. It is also an opportunity for you to heal a disconnection with your student and quickly manage the conflict.

Let's take a scenario where you promised the student that you would stay after and help, but you completely forgot. Unfortunately, to make matters worse, this is the second time an issue has occurred with this student and not making time to help them. The student is visibly frustrated, and it is time to act.

First, we need to *create*. We need to create the space, time, and opportunity to discuss the current issue. We need to ask the student to sit down and open ourselves up to create a common space for discussion. This is where you also *create* a sincere apology. This is a situation where you need to take ownership for what has happened and authentically show some remorse. If you create the space, time, and the opportunity for a genuine apology to occur, you can get the boat to shore safely. The repair has not started, but you know that you will not drown.

Next, we need to *uncover*. Even after the apology and openness for discussion have been created, that does not mean the student is going to be a willing participant. It is your obligation to *uncover* the meaning behind why they are upset. This means you will need to openly ask questions and find out what upset them the most. This part is critical because if you immediately try to come up with a solution for *connection*, you will be fixing a hole that might not need additional attention.

Maybe you believe that the student is upset because they feel like they are falling behind, and you provide another opportunity to meet with them. Then they say "No," and they exit. This means you did not *uncover* the real issue. You must find out. Maybe in this case, they were upset because they felt you didn't care about them because you accidentally forgot twice. This is the repair that needs to be *uncovered*. You know when you find it because the emotions will reveal themselves and they will begin to explain to you why they are upset. Stay calm; this is a good thing. This means the dialogue can begin again and the door to *connection* and *trust* is open.

Next, you must *reconsider* your approach moving forward. You must have the discussion with the student to find a mutually beneficial solution toward better change. For example, you are going to tell him/her that you have set alarms on your phone the next time this occurs, and that he/she may need to remind you the first time. The fact is that you need to make the adjustment and *reconsider* the methods in how you get that done.

Lastly, you must *express* that you value the dynamic of your relationship. You must be genuine in mentioning that you are creating this change to show them they matter. This *expression* means that you are ready to act and take the ship back on water. If *connection* and *trust* are about creating a deeper value, then *expressing* that value explicitly shows them you are back to full investment.

It should be noted that acting on that expression is equally critical. If you just took the time for investment and then did not follow through, the damage is much greater. Make sure you demonstrate commitment to follow through. That will be the first bond created moving forward.

CURE is a critical tactic to take a difficult situation and heal the underlying issues between two people. Notice what is still present in this: GAS. It requires genuine, actionable steps to accomplish getting through this tough scenario.

Creating the space is a genuine approach to allow meaningful action to occur. If authentic, the step of *Uncovering* provides enquiry-based learning to discover what is truly hurting them. *Reconsidering* is a tangible thought process that enables the other person to see you wanting to change. *Expressing* is a vocal action that genuinely ensures that you are going to move forward with the person, and not against them.

CURE is meant to be emergency repair. It provides the opportunity for you to move quickly to assess and heal the broken *connection*. It takes preparation, active listening, and an authentic willingness to want to fix the situation and re-establish *trust*. GAS must be utilized, or else CURE is simply a patch on a massive hole in your ship.

A Final Note about The Voyage Outward:
Be Human with your Acronym!

The Voyage Outward is about going deeper in your interactions than you could ever expect. I discussed in The Voyage Inward that building your acronym would function as your compass and always guide you in the right direction. One addition I would like to request when creating your acronym is to *be human* with it.

I have found over the last decade and a half that the educators who connect on the deepest level allow themselves to be human. Not only do they know the educator they are, they fully embrace it, and they get their students to embrace it as well. They know the content is valuable to establish credibility, but their *captivation*, *clarity*, and *connection* in the way they communicate with their audience is where long-term relationships are built.

I mentioned earlier in this book that "Fake it until you make it" does not fly with me. That is an archaic way to look at modern education. I am a firm believer in the idea that if you are human and your students see who you are as a human being, they will join you on The Voyage Outward. They will be *captivated* by what you share, they will be *clear* in what goals you want them to achieve and what needs must be addressed to get there, and they will be *connected* to you as a confidant, counselor, and coach.

I truly admire those who find *connection* through content and discussion alone because that is a gift. These educators have a keen wisdom for going as far as they can go to search for content. For me, I prefer to search as far as I can go to find identity. My identity. The student's individual identity, and our identity together in the classroom environment.

I have found that my deepest *connections* occur when I openly share something with them, and then get them to openly share something that they would have never expected when class began. This is an extremely vulnerable moment that occurs, and I always genuinely praise them for being so transparent.

This does not mean that you openly share every feeling you have ever felt in your entire life. Make sure you have some self-regulation. However, *connection* requires you to take a leap of faith in the way you interact with the student. It requires you to be vulnerable with taking chances. It requires you to be human.

This takes us to the end of The Voyage Outward. There is one final voyage to take, and ironically, this voyage does not end. We are going to embark The Voyage Beyond and sail on the final "C" – *Completeness*. It's time to go beyond the horizon!

CHAPTER 10:
THE VOYAGE BEYOND AND THE
SEVENTH "C" – COMPLETENESS

We have been on quite an adventure so far. We have learned how to recognize our inner strengths and areas of growth, how confidence impacts our practice, and how to engage the whole audience while meaningfully connecting with each person. Why does it still feel like there is still a missing piece? When you have sailed two entirely vast waters, what is left for an educator? The answer is *completeness*.

The "C" of *completeness* is a voyage you take when you apply everything you have learned and adapt it to your dynamics. This requires you to not only look inward and outward; it requires you to go beyond the teachings and start applying in your specific environments. Therefore, we are embarking on our final voyage. This is The Voyage Beyond.

The Voyage Beyond is not about knowing *what you do* for a living, it is about knowing *who you are*. It is one thing to grasp the concepts in this book; it is another to fully embrace how these concepts are going to make you the type of educator you aspire to be.

For example, if you had to answer these questions in detail, could you do it? These questions summarize the total experience:

1. What are your three greatest strengths as an educator, and do they apply to how you conduct your *delivery, style, transparency,* and *modality? (Command)*

2. What are your three greatest weaknesses you know you can change regarding your *delivery, style, transparency,* and *modality?* What adjustments do you need to make? *(Change)*

3. What proof do you have of how you demonstrate each strength or change? How many times have you practiced these strategies, and how confident are you in your discipline to apply? *(Confidence)*

4. What are your best strategies to engage your audience as a whole, and how often have you tried each? *(Captivation)*

5. How clear is your message that the information and presentation of the material is going to benefit your students personally? *(Clarity)*

6. What are your go-to's to build more meaningful trust with each student in your classroom environment? *(Connection)*

If you are still having difficulty with any of these questions, believe me, that's more than okay. This book is meant to be a constant review of who you want to become, and that is why The Voyage Beyond is so critical. It requires you to continuously re-evaluate your approaches and ensure you are still the best educator you possibly can be.

How many times have you seen an educator that used to be amazing years ago and is still teaching the same exact way they did twenty years later? Are they still as effective?

The answer is most likely no. Educational strategies change. The research changes. The technology changes. The societal values change. Most importantly, the students change. If you do not change, then you will be left behind.

Every time you teach a new class, you have a new experience that requires you to evaluate your current methods and evolve your approach. This is a perfect opportunity to check your current practices and see what works and what doesn't. The best educators know that they must go *beyond* who they were as an educator to still find who they want to become. They constantly go on The Voyage Beyond and sail on the "C" to ensure *completeness* in their practices. That is what makes them the best.

Nearly fifteen years later, I still tell myself I must do this. I now teach leadership and development courses that are one-day to five-day classes, which means my students change immensely and often. If I did not re-evaluate my teaching constantly, I would fall into the same cycle. As I am writing this book, I still take the journey on the seventh "C" and occasionally jump to another "C" when I feel I am missing something. More on that in a bit.

Conquering The Voyage Beyond by Conquering your Fears

The Voyage Beyond is about conquering what you have not faced yet. There will be adventures down the road that will require you to check yourself as an educator. The more proactive you are, the better the outcome.

The most significant aspect behind The Voyage Beyond is that when you do check yourself, you must recognize the two-headed creature that lurks below the surface, known as Fear. The reason this creature is two-headed is because there are two disastrous fears that can take you under at any moment: Fear of the Unknown and Fear of Failure.

These two fears are the reason that many people fear death, heights, public speaking, drowning, spiders, and more. First, we have no idea what the outcomes are going to be, and because of this, we play about a trillion different scenarios in our heads and make ourselves fearful. We simply fear what we do not know. Second, we fear that when we lose control, we will essentially fail. We talk ourselves out of situations because if we fail, we will be alone. In the field of Education, either one of these fears can cause an educator to stress themselves to no return and simply sink to the bottom.

The Voyage Beyond is about never stopping in your pursuit of excellence. It is about looking for ways to advance yourself to find *completeness* in your abilities. This is the exact reason why these two concepts fall in one chapter. The only way you find *completeness* as an educator is to go beyond in your research, practices, evaluation, and self-reflection.

The "C" of Completeness

Completeness is the state of being complete. *Being complete.* There is a reason I did not choose *completion*. There are vast differences.

First, when you have *completeness*, you are *being* complete in your practices. Completion is the finishing of tasks. *Completeness* is the understanding that you are complete as an educator. You know your methods inside and out. You can read your audience and anticipate their needs before they even recognize them. You have reached the deepest level of self-efficacy so that you know the next move at precisely the right time.

Second, and most important, you can be in a state of *completeness* and still have the desire to search for more information, whereas completion means you have finished and can sit down. *Completeness* is the concept whereby you can seek new information while knowing yourself and how you can further your knowledge, skills, and applications. It does not mean you are weak or are missing anything; it simply means you are constantly growing, and you know that growth becomes a part of who you are. The Voyage Beyond is not a scary adventure to you anymore; you find *completeness* in the voyage itself.

The greatest explorers of all time believed that there were always new waters to discover and it became their life mission. The best educators do the same. I have never heard an amazing 30-year educator ever say, "This is the way we have always done it." One of the best quotes came from a mentor of mine when I was first teaching, when she said, "The moment you think you know it all, get out of teaching." To me, she is the epitome of *completeness*. She could dock the ship at shore, and no one would ever question her integrity. She stayed out there because she always believes there is more to find.

Completeness is also crucial because the field of Education changes incredibly fast. Techniques and initiatives change yearly. That is the main reason that this book doesn't focus on techniques or initiatives. It focuses on mindsets, principles, and internal values. Those are timeless anchors. If you are going to navigate waters that are calm one day and choppy the next, you must be able to have anchors to help you weather the changing storms.

The number one goal of this chapter is to stay firm and strong in your belief that you can always learn something new, try something new, and practice something new. It is a crucial skill that allows us to be ahead of the teaching game. More importantly, it keeps us positive when the storms smack us. This is the definition of *completeness* because it ensures that with a positive, steady mindset there is always something out there to help us grow. The answer is never *no*, it is *not yet*.

Lastly, *completeness* is about ensuring that you have time for meta-reflection. This is the ability to gain awareness of your own awareness in how you can grow. It is one thing to actively learn a new concept; it is another to understand how that concept can help you with the strengths you already possess and the changes you need to make.

For example, I recently learned a new concept in a book by Jeb Blount, titled *Objections: The Art and Science of Getting Past No*. His concept is simple: "*If you do not ask, you will not get.*" What an incredibly powerful idea this is because it promotes a sense of always looking for the next option to grow!

This is an amazing belief system for an educator to have because it requires you to not be afraid to ask the questions necessary to get the answers you desire. Here is the question I have for you: How does actively asking questions help you as the educator you are versus the educator you want to be?

For me, I needed to learn that I assume a bit too much in my teaching practices and though my instincts are fairly on point, I am wrong from time to time. I needed to learn to ask better engagement questions for deeper reflection about what information I can gain. I now include more engaging questions about self-reflection for students in my teaching because I have found that they learn more about themselves than they ever expected.

This is a prime example of what *completeness* can be. It's not just about learning the concept; it is about finding how that concept can enhance your teaching practices and keep you relevant in an ever-changing adventure. Even after a decade and a half, I still can learn something new, find value in the practice, and execute it based on my style of teaching. It is revitalizing as an educator, and it keeps me wanting to research the next idea that can benefit my teaching practices.

One lurking question I still ask myself is, "Why do teachers stop this pursuit of enhancing their teaching practices?" The only answer that I have found are The Fear Storms: *The Fear of Change* and *The Fear of the Unknown*.

Conquering The Fear Storms

For the last fifteen years, I have watched amazing teachers, professors, and educators leave the profession. I have conducted years' worth of research on this and the same answer appears: *Burnout*. Education is a draining profession because we put our heads, hearts, and souls into this. Over time, we exhaust ourselves to the point where we have nothing left in the tank. Many educators believe that burnout comes from stress, which I wholeheartedly agree.

The question that no one asks is, "How do we reduce this stress?" What I have found is that the only answer is recognizing, confronting, and working through our fears.

Fear functions like a storm in the ocean; the waters appear to be calm, and suddenly, thunder, lightning, high seas, and damage occurs. Next thing you know, your boat is sinking and you have lost all drive as an educator. The two biggest storms that challenge them are fear of the unknown and fear of change.

After looking closely at the educators who have weathered the storms, they have all done the same thing: They conquered these two storms.

It took me a long time to find out how. First, they actively and positively seek anything that is *unknown*. Therefore *completeness* is critical. It puts our frame of reference in a place that says, "It's okay that we do not have 100% of the answers. We will find them and make a difference." It is unwaveringly positive and motivating.

Consequently, it is not easy. It requires us to not beat ourselves up. It requires us to make sure that we recognize that over time, our changes will impact others. It requires us to have positive shields against the turbulent waters. As educators, we need to know that what we are doing is truly impactful and that we will find the answers to make a difference in our students' lives. If you have read this far, I will tell you this: *You will make it happen. You always do and you always will.*

Second, these elite educators do not just embrace change, they *seek* it. They want to be the first to try new things. They are willing to take the risk to understand the concept better and want to go for it. It is truly uplifting.

Again, this is not easy. It requires us to shift our mindsets from a place of *Succeed or Fail* to *Succeed or Learn*. With every metric, score, observation, evaluation, comments, initiative, and everything else that education and training throw our way, it becomes that much more important to believe that you are not failing. You are learning, and with that learning comes greater meaning and impact that you will change lives. Much like the first fear, I will tell you this one more time: *You will make it happen. You always do and you always will.*

We can become our own worst enemies and my goal is to remind you that you entered this profession for a reason. We need to go back to that reason to understand the answers we are seeking. I entered education to make a meaningful impact every day for the students I teach. I lost this belief once and it caused me to leave. When I got back into the educational realm, I found it again, and this time I have not let it go. Since then, everything that I have researched, learned, practiced, or deployed has followed under that premise. Believe me when I tell you that it has made all the difference.

One final note about The Fear Storms: They pass. The lack of understanding and lack of wanting to change goes away and the skies become much clearer. It requires you to have the mindset of *completeness* because we make the unknown known and we make change a daily practice. When we have a sense of *completeness*, this allows us to shift our mindset to understand that there is always room for growth, and we will always figure it out. Once we have obtained that mindset, everything else becomes positively clear. When we go with the waters (instead of against them), we find that they are a lot less choppy.

A final important concept of this chapter is this: When we feel we are completely lost at sea and the waters feel unforgiving, we must always anchor ourselves back to the preparation of CYA. We must re-evaluate how we thoroughly prepare the components of *Our Content, Ourselves*, and *Our Audience*. Let's show you how to meaningfully conduct this anchoring process and get back to shore safely.

Anchoring Back to CYA

We began with the value of preparing differently, and we will finish with the value of preparing differently. We must ensure we have our final checklist of preparation complete every time we are ready to embark on a new voyage. CYA allows us to make sure that before we go off into the distance, we are not doing it without our maps and compass to guide us through.

Let's briefly review the CYA Model of Preparation one more time:

Figure 5: The CYA Model of Preparation

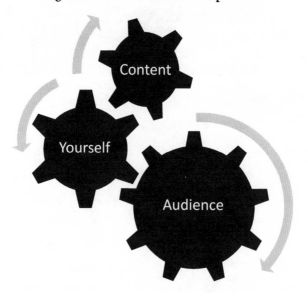

I emphasized the importance of not only preparing your content but preparing yourself for meaningful delivery and preparing for your audience's needs and goals. This does not mean that you neglect your content. The content is your key to demonstrating credible knowledge.

In fact, without all three of the pieces working together, your preparation will feel disjointed and will not carry you as far as you would like to go. They are the pieces of the motor that allow your ship to move in the first place.

We have spent time unpacking the twelve components of CYA, broken down in Chapters 1 (Content), 3 (Yourself), and 6 (Audience). When you are getting ready to take another voyage beyond on the "C" of Completeness, you must make sure that you have *everything* you could need and *anything* you might not need. Being holistic with your approach is the only way that you can venture into something new and gain meaning from it.

Table 9 below allows you to run through an educational checklist to make sure you have prepared for anything that could occur. It confirms that you have found new *content* to master, new methods to try *yourself,* and new techniques to build belief within your *audience*. It is imperative that anytime you are ready to try something new beyond your scope, you prepare all twelve components appropriately.

Table 9: The CYA Model of Preparation for All Components

Content (Already Gained)	Yourself (Voyage Inward)	Audience (Voyage Outward)
Substance	*Delivery*	*Engagement*
Elaboration	*Style*	*Depth*
Relevant Examples	*Transparency*	*Alignment*
Real-World Application	*Modality*	*Trust*

The twelve components focus on your ability to make the content meaningful and applicable, your approach to demonstrating power through your teaching design, and your lasting impression on your audience. To do this all at once can be exhausting and arduous, especially if you are on a time-crunch, you do not feel comfortable with the technology, or your mind is not in the right space. This requires total focus to truly identify and utilize new information in a way that will leave a meaningful impact on your learners.

As I have mentioned throughout, I am not leaving you in open waters. Appendix D will be one final emergency equipment kit to make you feel safer and more confident in your ability to prepare more effectively. I call this emergency kit the *CYA Anchor Guide* (Next Page). This holistic guide provides you with the listed twelve components, valuable questions to ask, and the information you need to provide. When completed, it will not feel like completion; it will feel like *completeness*. It will feel like you have scoured every inch of the educational world to bring better meaning to others.

However, I must stress this: The *CYA Anchor Guide* should only be used as a replacement of the *TMS's* or *IROS Organizers* when you completely understand who you are as an educator. Completing this guide before understanding *TMS's and* the *IROS Organizers* is basically like learning to run before trying to crawl or walk. The *CYA Anchor Guide* is meant for those who legitimately know who they are as an educator and are looking for a deeper conscious practice. With enough repetitions over time, it will become a second-nature walk-through that can be done as a routine.

My advice is to first begin with the *TMS's* and the *IROS Organizers* to gain a deeper understanding of your approaches, and then to think about and utilize the *CYA Anchor Guide* as the quest to expand your horizons on greater learning, meaning, and efficacy. The guide is not for novices who are learning to navigate the open seas, but rather for expert captains who are seeking the highest level of certification that allows you to sail anywhere you would like.

In this table, I have provided a detailed example as a walkthrough of all twelve components, as shown in C, Y, then A format:

Table 10: CYA Anchor Guide

Concept to Learn: Teaching others to teach online more effectively through Microsoft TEAMS		
CYA Component	**Question to Ask**	**Answer**
Substance (C)	What can this concept do for other people if understood clearly?	**Microsoft TEAMS can help teachers comfortably teach synchronously and asynchronously to help their students share information more effectively.**
Elaboration (C)	How can this information be broken down to help others understand it?	**Microsoft TEAMS provides channels, sharing of documents, chat, meetings, videos, and more in one collaborative space. Each needs to be learned and demonstrated for others.**
Relevant Example (C)	What is a key example that students could make connections?	**For example, if I needed to teach trainers how to teach using Microsoft TEAMS, I would provide the example of setting up a TEAMS invite through Outlook, connecting, and recording the meeting to show engagement.**

Real-World Application (C)	How can students take this information and make meaning in their own lives?	This feature can be applied when facilitators are teaching others to use the program effectively, while still helping their teaching practices.
Delivery (Y)	How are you going to deliver this message to students?	Lecture first, demonstration/modeling second, practice together third, breakouts fourth, review and takeaways last.
Style (Y)	What style of teaching are you going to approach with?	The style will be built around empowerment and connection. I am going to be serious but electrifying to have them get excited and personal with their own learning.
Transparency (Y)	How open are you going to be with them?	Very transparent. I am going to share that I had fears myself in the beginning because it was an all-in-one solution. But I am going to show them how awesome it is to use!
Modality (Y)	How is this going to be delivered? F2F? Online?	Online Synchronous at first, and if they have the software to practice later, I am going to give them an asynchronous assignment to practice and share.
Engagement (A)	How are you going to initially captivate your audience?	I am going to create an initial Outlook invite with a TEAMS link and show them how to get in. Once they are in, I am going to wear something hilarious in the beginning to get them excited about the webcams. From there, I will share something equally funny to show them that humor can be driven through this type of lesson.
Depth (A)	How are you going to deep-dive from there?	I am going to explain the video feature and share screen feature to them and have them practice turning it on. Then, I am going to let them hang up the call and practice separately with an assigned partner. They are each going to practice and come back to show depth.

Alignment (A)	How are you going to align yourself to them?	I am going to mess up something intentionally to show them when they come back that it is okay to make a mistake. I want them to know that we all have bumps, but it is working through those bumps that give us greater efficacy.
Trust (A)	How are you going to have them open up to you and build trust?	I am going to have them open up their initial fears and ask them how they worked through the roadblocks. Once one person shares, I am going to praise them genuinely to show them how much their share truly means. This will engage others to want to openly share too.

The *CYA Anchor Guide* propels you to investigate yourself quickly and efficiently. It allows you to go through your progressions, navigate your components, and propel you forward with new ideas. If you don't have an answer to a question, skip it for the time being and come back when you have a fresh new idea.

The reason why the *CYA Anchor Guide* asks these specific questions is because you already know who you are as an educator and it steers the ship for you when you feel a bit off course. This activity is meant to search for completeness is because you would already have full awareness of each component and the power that they bring. Therefore, asking the questions as a simple reminder for you to specify and elaborate more quickly. The progression you go through with this guide is meant to review a checklist before deciding on a new adventure. It is not meant to create a whole new discovery and for you to spend countless hours reflecting on your practices.

With that being stated, you could still choose to be as explicit and detailed with your answers as you would like. If you wanted to use it to answer more deeply, you have that option. If you want to use this as a lesson plan, technically, you could do that effectively as well. It is truly meant to capture your drive as the brilliant educator that you are and allow you to seek new opportunities more easily.

A Final Note on The Voyage Beyond

When you are navigating this final "C" on The Voyage Beyond, you get to decide how deep and how far you would like to venture. This ultimately becomes your journey. That's the beauty of striving for a meaningful life as an educator; you get to choose your own adventure and decide where you want to go next. Remember, *you are the captain of your ship.*

Sometimes, this voyage will feel like you are getting knocked off course. That's okay. If we have learned one thing about this voyage, it is that it's not about the destination, it is about the journey. Remember to allow yourself to reflect occasionally. Take in the air, the scenery, the experience, and the memories. These will be the motivators to try something new and venture further into the great unknown that is the teaching experience.

This is what creates *completeness.* Everyone's Voyage Beyond is uniquely different and the possibilities are endless. You get to look back, live in the present, and look forward all at once. You get to build your body of work, your way.

Now that we have a new profound sense of *completeness,* it is time to allow you to take control of the ship and sail off on your own voyage!

CONCLUSION:
PLOTTING YOUR COURSE
AND TAKING THE HELM

Wow! We have worked so well together, and you have now brought the ship back to shore. You are ready to begin your own voyages. Now that we have explored all seven "C's" together, it is time to begin setting sail.

But where to begin? There seems to be so much to apply. Remember the old adage of "taking one bite at a time." These voyages are not meant to be short lived. There is a reason the concepts in the book can help you for years to come. It is because these concepts are meant for you to work on one thing at a time and master it.

The trick to any voyage is plotting your course in advance. It is about knowing where you have been, what you have tried, where you currently stand as an educator, what you want to look like as an educator, and how you get there. These steps are extremely self-reflective, and you must be truly honest with yourself.

Once you have taken some time to understand who you are and who you want to be, it is time to put the steps to action. First, make sure you know how you want to map your course and provide yourself with a clear, actionable direction to take. Fortunately, I have provided you with a map to help you plot your course more easily and effectively, so that you can remind yourself of where you currently are in the process. Actually, let's call it your MAPS.

Plotting Your Course with MAPS

First, I use the acronym MAPS because you are going on three different voyages and seven different "C's" by yourself. It is only fitting that you apply different strategies along the way. Second, MAPS stands for: *Model* (Preparation), *Ask* (Questions about Yourself), *Plan* (A Route to Each of Your Audience Members), and *Set* (A Cyclical Process for Future Learning).

Each step is there to help you to prepare your ship, navigate the waters of The Voyage Inward and The Voyage Outward, and venture as far as you possibly can on The Voyage Beyond. These steps include:

1. Model all preparation around CYA. Study all twelve components of the *CYA Model of Preparation* and get to know how you can use each to prepare your content, yourself, and your audience for better instruction.

   - Content: Substance, Elaboration, Relevant Examples, Real-world Application

   - Yourself: Your Delivery, Your Style, Your Transparency, Your Use of Modality

   - Audience: Engagement, Depth, Alignment, Trust

2. Ask questions about who you are as an educator. Use the *TMS-Statements* to understand how you can connect all four pieces of yourself in the skills you have and the changes you need. (Voyage Inward)

   - Where do you have amazing command of your teaching?

   - Where you need to make significant changes?

   - What technological platforms are you using to teach, and how can you make your teaching approach enhance the environment?

   - How can you set up a plan to practice and make changes to your course?

3. Plan to understand what makes every audience member tick and adjust your course of teaching around them and use the *IROS Organizer* to document (Voyage Outward).

   - What ideas and activities can captivate them and give you their undivided attention?

   - How can you take those ideas and provide deeper meaning to have them truly grasp the concept?

   - How can you align the ideas to their overall purpose for learning? What do they get out of it?

   - How do you get them to trust that you are the person who can guide them in the right direction?

4. Set a cyclical review process to understand where you can continue to grow. Once you have gained efficacy in your ability to change other's lives, go through a faster manner in your preparation techniques by utilizing the *CYA Anchor Guide* (Voyage Beyond).

   - Always look for something new to learn and practice.

   - Self-assess your current techniques, practice self-discipline in learning new ideas, and gain efficacy in the skill until it becomes second-nature.

Taking the Helm

These approaches will be constant reminders of which steps in the voyage you need to plan or readjust. It is now up to you to work through each process and truly meta-reflect on the way you are approaching the educational realm, both in a F2F and online platform. This is known as *Taking the Helm*.

I mentioned in the last chapter that no one else is the captain of your ship. *You are the captain of your ship.* The beauty of great education is that it is potentially limitless. The only limitation that can be created comes from your own mind. The more you grip the wheel and hold firm, the better you will become.

If you need additional guidance, you have the appendices in the back of the book to remind you where you need to go. Make as many copies as you need to help you identify areas for educational growth. Use them as the buoys to make sure you are not running into hazards as you are navigating the choppy waters.

I wish you nothing but success on your voyages. I know that my voyages have taught me more than I could have ever imagined. Using these models, statements, organizers, and additional tools have shaped me into the educator I want to be. They have allowed me to efficiently reflect and make more meaningful changes. I know there is always open space to sail on that seventh "C" of *completeness*, but I feel more and more comfortable every day and it shows in the feedback I receive from students. I know that by faithfully practicing, you will gather those same feelings that I live every day in my teaching.

With that said, it is time for you to take the helm! Goodbye, good luck, and Godspeed to you on your upcoming voyages!

APPENDIX A:

THE VOYAGE INWARD – STRENGTHENING TEACHER MINDSET STATEMENT (S-TMS) TEMPLATE

Complete each section in the table by completing this mad-lib: **If I am/ possess/have** _____ *(Strength)*, **I would/should/can** _____ *(Action that supports strength)* **into my educational lesson to ensure better** _____ *(Delivery/Style/Transparency/Modality)*. **This will make me a better educator because** _____ *(Reason that supports strength)*.

Delivery	*Style*
Yourself: Major Strength _____	
Transparency	*Modality*

APPENDIX B:
THE VOYAGE INWARD – CHANGING TEACHER MINDSET STATEMENT (C-TMS) TEMPLATE

Complete each section in the table by completing this mad-lib: **If I do not possess/have** _____ *(Strength)*, **I would/should/can** _____ *(Action that engages change)* **into my educational lesson to ensure better** _____ *(Delivery/Style/Transparency/Modality)*. **This will make me a better educator because** _____ *(Reason that supports strength)*.

Delivery	*Style*
Yourself: Major Weakness _____	
Transparency	*Modality*

APPENDIX C:

THE VOYAGE OUTWARD – IDEAS, REFLECTIONS, OBSERVATIONS AND STATEMENTS (IROS) TEMPLATE

Version (Attempt)	Audience Component	Idea (I)	Reflection (R)	Observations (O)	Statements of Similarities or Differences (S)

APPENDIX D:
THE VOYAGE BEYOND – CYA ANCHOR GUIDE TEMPLATE

Concept to Learn:		
CYA Component	**Question to Ask**	**Answer**
Substance (Content)	What can this concept do for other people if understood clearly?	
Elaboration (Content)	How can this information be broken down to help others understand it?	
Relevant Example (Content)	What is a key example that students could make connections?	
Real-World Application (Content)	How can students take this information and make meaning in their own lives?	
Delivery (Yourself)	How are you going to deliver this message to students?	

Style (Yourself)	What style of teaching are you going to approach with?	
Transparency (Yourself)	How open are you going to be with them?	
Modality (Yourself)	How is this going to be delivered? F2F? Online?	
Engagement (Audience)	How are you going to initially captivate your audience?	
Depth (Audience)	How are you going to deep-dive from there?	
Alignment (Audience)	How are you going to align yourself to them?	
Trust (Audience)	How are you going to have them open up to you and build trust?	

INDEX

A

Acronym
> 65, 66, 112, 114, 131, 140

Activity
> 13, 50, 52–56, 71, 72, 79, 81–87, 94, 95, 128, 140

Adobe
> 8, 140

Alignment
> 15, 17, 23, 69, 70, 76, 78, 79, 84–87, 90, 91, 93–97, 100, 101, 104, 107–9, 125, 128, 131, 139, 140

Amoeba
> 27, 140

Anchor
> 79, 92, 123, 125, 126, 128, 132, 138, 140

Approach
> 2, 5, 9, 12–14, 16, 18, 26, 28, 31–36, 42, 44, 46, 50, 52, 58, 59, 63, 72, 83, 91, 104, 108, 113, 117, 124, 125, 127, 131, 139, 140

Asynchronous
> 1, 2, 26, 127, 140

Audience

9, 13–15, 17, 18, 23, 26, 31, 33, 37–43, 51–53, 66–72, 74, 76–80, 82–85, 87–94, 96, 97, 100–102, 105, 107, 108, 110, 111, 114, 116, 117, 119, 123–25, 127, 131, 132, 136, 139

Authentic

13, 36, 39, 43, 50, 66, 93, 109, 113, 141

B

Breakout

35, 50, 54, 55, 84, 91–93, 96, 141

Burnout

28, 121, 141

C

Captivation

4, 68, 70, 72, 76–80, 82–87, 89–92, 100–102, 105, 114, 117, 141

Change

3, 4, 7, 20–22, 25–27, 32, 40, 44–48, 50–57, 61–63, 65, 68, 73, 78, 80, 83, 100, 113, 117, 118, 120–23, 132, 135, 141

Clarity

4, 61, 68, 70, 73, 76, 78, 88–97, 100–102, 104, 114, 117, 141

Classroom

9, 16, 21, 30, 34, 36, 39, 42, 43, 48, 49, 60, 91, 96, 102, 109, 114, 117, 141

Command

3, 4, 21, 22, 25, 27, 29–33, 36–40, 42, 43, 48, 52, 64, 65, 68, 73, 79, 80, 83, 84, 100, 117, 131, 141

Commitment

97, 104, 113, 141

F

Face-to-face

2, 14, 17, 42, 144

Facilitation

2, 94, 144

Facilitator

19, 95, 96, 144

Failure

28, 61, 118, 144

Fear

51, 61, 106, 118, 121–23, 144

Feedback

1, 5, 19, 27, 42, 46, 47, 49, 53, 54, 71, 74, 83–85, 93, 133, 144

G

GAS

101–6, 108–10, 113, 144

GoToWebinar

8, 144

Group

11, 12, 16, 28, 33, 35, 48, 50, 65, 75, 81, 82, 86, 91–95, 97, 100, 144

Growth

5, 7, 17, 22, 27–29, 50, 53, 58, 59, 73–76, 80, 85, 90, 100, 116, 119, 123, 133, 144

H

Hands-on

12, 33, 35, 48, 144

K

Knowledge

2, 5, 7, 10, 12, 31, 68, 75, 89, 102, 103, 108, 119, 124, 145

L

Learning

1–3, 5, 6, 8, 12, 14, 18, 33, 34, 36, 42, 45, 48, 51, 55, 65, 68, 73, 74, 77–81, 84, 100, 110, 113, 121, 122, 125–27, 131, 132, 146

Lesson

12, 14, 15, 17, 25, 28, 31, 32, 34, 37, 39, 47, 48, 50, 51, 62–64, 68, 69, 71, 77–79, 81, 82, 84, 86, 89, 95, 127, 128, 134, 135, 146

LinkedIn

1, 146

LMS

8, 146

M

Management

8, 16, 24, 146

Maslow

2, 146

Mastery

11, 13, 18, 22, 44, 63–65, 69, 146

Meaning

4, 5, 19, 22, 31, 35, 51, 53–56, 58, 59, 68, 70, 80, 83, 84, 87, 92, 95, 96, 102–4, 108, 112, 122, 124–27, 132, 138, 146

Meeting

15, 56, 61, 87, 126, 146

S

T

U

Understand

7, 8, 10, 12, 16–20, 24, 29, 39, 44–46, 49, 66, 67, 73, 79, 91, 96, 120, 122, 123, 125, 130–32, 138, 152

Unwavering

5, 43, 152

V

Values

3, 4, 21, 22, 24, 26, 31–33, 44, 78, 89, 90, 97, 117, 120, 152

Voyage

3–6, 12, 15, 19, 21–23, 28, 29, 44, 45, 56, 57, 59, 64–69, 71, 74, 75, 79, 80, 85, 87–89, 95, 114–19, 123–25, 129–32, 152

Vulnerability

16, 70, 104–6, 152

W

Weakness

24, 45, 47, 49, 51–56, 73, 80, 135, 152

Weaknesses

4, 16, 21, 25–27, 33, 44–46, 53, 56, 117, 152

Webcam

16, 41, 152

Web-conference

42, 152

WebEx

8, 152

Wheel

4, 9, 22, 23, 30–32, 40, 71, 133, 153